THE CHILD SUPPORT DEFICIT

Where Policy Meets Parenthood

by

Eshe Oluchi

The Art of Eshe Publishing

© 2025

For information, contact:

The Art of Eshe Publishing

[you can add your website or business address here later]

ISBN: [leave blank until you register]

First Edition: 2025

Cover and interior design by *The Art of Eshe*

Dedication

To the fathers who stayed. To the mothers who carried the weight.

To the children who deserved more, and the communities who refused to give up.

May this book be a light, a truth, and a healing tool for generations to come.

To my parents,

Thank you for the consistency, love, and dedication that you've shown me. I learned that I don't have to be perfect, but I do have to be present. You taught me loyalty to my children and my lineage. I am forever grateful for the support that you have given to me and my boys.

To my family,

To anyone in my family that has ever supported me, I am infinitely grateful. I love you and may God bless you abundantly for stepping in for me and mine.

To my sons,

May God help you to keep your hearts pure and kind. God. Boundaries. Self reflection. Self-love. Saying Thank You. This will be your greatest ally for growth and protection. Do what is right even when no one is looking. Living in integrity is the gift of peace. It frees you from having to lie to other people and yourself. It keeps you from always looking over your shoulder, and from living in your head. Remember that no one can take what is in your mind if you don't allow them to get into your head. This world is so beautiful and big. Don't get stuck in the negative things. Be happy and do the things that give you peace.

I love you

Mom

TaBLe OF Contents

Chapter 1

The Kingdom Belongs to Such as These

Before you read a single word, pause. Listen to the part of you that already knows this was never just about money. It's about presence. About absence. About the unseen weight we carry and the legacy we're called to build.

The power of a father isn't just measured by what he provides but by what he protects. It's not about money. It's about presence, influence, spiritual order, and the integrity he brings into a space. A father sets the tone, and when he's missing, when that energy is absent, you can feel the void.

There are so many young men out here searching for themselves, not because they're weak, but because nobody ever stood before them and said, *"You are enough."* Nobody showed them how to walk as a man without ego, how to cry without shame, how to love without control. And the cost of that absence ripples through communities, through generations.

Our fathers weren't perfect, but they were our first mirrors. Some showed us our strength; some showed us our wounds. But either way, they left us with a choice: repeat or rebuild. Being a man is not about dominance; it's about responsibility. It's about standing firm in who you are so that others can rest in who they are. It's about protecting what's sacred: family, peace, order. It's knowing when to be strong and when to be still, when to fight and when to walk away, when to lead and when to listen.

There is power in the masculine, not the corrupted, performative version the world tries to sell us. I'm talking about divine masculine energy: the kind that covers, the kind that builds, the kind that doesn't have to prove itself because it simply *is*. The kind that walks into a room and restores balance.

To the man who didn't show up: this isn't a story of blame. It's a story of what your absence has taught. Because even a shadow can teach you where the light belongs. We live in a time where so many are trying to redefine or reject what it means to be a man, but the truth is, real manhood never needed a rebrand. It just needed to be remembered. It needed to be witnessed. And the ones who were raised without it, we see everything. We see the cracks, the strain, the way mothers had to overcompensate, the way children carry questions they never had the words to ask. And some of us decided that we would break that cycle.

This isn't about perfection. It's about intention. It's about honesty. It's about a man saying, "I don't have it all together, but I'm here. I'm learning. I'm trying." That kind of humility? That's powerful. That's healing. Fathers matter. Not just the ones who show up on paper, but the ones who show up in spirit. The ones who stay when it's hard. The ones who apologize when they're wrong. The ones who show their sons how to love and their daughters what to expect.

It's time we honor that. It's time we build spaces where men can be seen, heard, and held accountable, with love. Where they can grow into their full selves without fear or shame. Because when a man is rooted, the whole family thrives. The whole community flourishes. And for those who never had that example? You can still become it. You can still change. You can still choose to be the father, the mentor, the protector you never had.

Some men become fathers through blood. Others become fathers through choice. In communities where absence has been the norm, the men who choose to stand in the gap are the ones who change everything. They coach the teams. They mentor the boys. They show up for the graduations, the hard talks, the quiet moments when someone just needs to be seen. That choice? That presence? That's divine.

We honor the men who didn't have to but did. The uncles, the grandfathers, the big brothers, the neighbors, the teachers, the ones who said, "I see you," and meant it. They are proof that fatherhood is not just a title, it's a calling. When men answer that call, entire generations rise. This is how we break generational curses. These are the kind of men I was raised around. Men who protected children and never harmed them. The kind who fed other people's kids just because they were there. Their blessings did not come from the people, but those men are blessed by God.

"Children are a heritage from the Lord, offspring a reward from him." — Psalm 127:3

"Whoever welcomes one of these little children in my name welcomes me; and whoever welcomes me does not welcome me but the one who sent me." — Mark 9:37

"Truly I tell you, unless you change and become like little children, you will never enter the kingdom of heaven." — Matthew 18:3

"Let the little children come to me, and do not hinder them, for the kingdom of God belongs to such as these." — Luke 18:16

Children carry the purest reflection of Heaven on Earth. And to care for them, to feed them, protect them, and to teach them is to honor the very essence of life itself. We are not just raising sons and daughters; we are stewarding souls. The men who understand this carry the real power. Not because they are perfect, but because they are present. This book is not a finger pointed. It's a light held up. It's a call to look deeper at the systems, the silence, the statistics, and the strength it takes to stand in the gap.

Chapter 2

Stop the Bleeding: Funding Families by Fixing What's Broken

Let's talk numbers. In **fiscal year 2022**, the U.S. government spent around **$119.4 billion** on SNAP—**$113.9 billion** in direct food benefits and **$5.5 billion** in administrative costs. By **2023**, that number dropped to **$112 billion**, and by **2024**, it slid to just over **$100.3 billion**.

Now compare that to the **$113 billion** in unpaid child support. That's money legally owed but never received. And when child support *is* collected, particularly in cases tied to public aid like TANF, **the government often keeps that**

money, claiming it as reimbursement. The custodial parent never sees it. The child still goes without.

What's worse, once the government garnishes those wages from the non-custodial parent, that parent no longer wants to, or can't help in other ways either. They can't cash app you. They can't send a Zelle. A lot of the time, they are then unwilling to send any money even if they have it. That money is gone—locked up in a system that takes from one parent, denies it to the other, and then blames both.

Meanwhile, lawmakers are calling for cuts to programs like Section 8 and SNAP at a time when people really need the help. The bigger truth: **the system already has money, it just refuses to give it to the families it's meant for.** If we stopped playing tug-of-war with survival and started funding families with the support they're already owed, we wouldn't need so many band-aid policies. Families would be more stable. Kids would be better off. And we could finally stop blaming the parents who stayed and start holding accountable

the systems, and the people that didn't.

Chapter 3

The Great Illusion: When Policy Ignores the Other Half

Let's be real. We are living inside a system where everyone is pretending like this is normal. Like it makes sense for one parent to carry the emotional, physical, and financial weight of raising a child while the other disappears into thin air. And the state? It just shrugs. Sometimes it even rewards the silence. This isn't just negligence. This is design. It's the illusion of balance in a system that's tilted on purpose. We get hit with policy after policy meant to punish, meant to discipline meant to push us into compliance. But where is the pressure on the other half? Where are the consequences when support doesn't come? When effort doesn't show up? When absence become routine?

Here's the math: parents across the U.S. are owed more than **$113 billion in unpaid child support**, and only about **40% of custodial parents ever see the full amount they're due**. Another third receives only partial payments, while **30% receive nothing at all**. That means billions of dollars meant to feed children and stabilize households simply vanish. It can be decades before the custodial parent receives back payment.

Meanwhile, the cost of raising a child keeps climbing. In 2024, it averaged **$21,681 per year per child**, a **19% increase since 2016**. For many families, that's the cost of rent, food, childcare, and health insurance combined. By the time a child turns 17, the total cost reaches nearly **$310,000**. And in places like Boston or San Francisco, annual costs top $39,000, more than some people's full salaries.

Yet, who shoulders the weight when support doesn't show up? Single mothers are five times more likely to live in poverty than married couples, with nearly 1 in 3 raising their children below the poverty line. And the disparities cut even deeper: more than 35% of Black and Hispanic single mothers live in poverty, compared to 20% of white single mothers.

We're told to keep our receipts. File our paperwork. Appear in court. Adjust our expectations. "Do it for the kids." And we do. We stretch. We sacrifice. We show up. Over and over again. But the illusion is starting to crack. Because here's the truth: there are solutions. We could ease the pressure if we really wanted to. If we collected child support and actually gave it to the families. If we stopped penalizing the poor for needing help while ignoring the wealthy politicians who hoard our resources. If we told the full truth, that the problem isn't just "absent fathers" or "lazy mothers," it's a system that refuses to hold the whole equation accountable. It's time to break the illusion.

Chapter 4

The Illusion of Enforcement

They say there's a system in place to ensure fairness. If someone doesn't pay child support, there are consequences. But here's what they don't tell you: enforcement is selective. It's loud when the non-custodial parent is low-income or easy to track. It's whisper-quiet when they're wealthy, self-employed, or know how to hide assets. Most men who do not pay their child support and are not incarcerated, have learned how to hide their money.

Even when there is enforcement, like garnished wages or intercepted tax refunds rarely bring consistency, and it never brings equity. On paper, the federal Office of Child

Support Enforcement reports over $30 billion collected each year, but less than two-thirds of that money ever reaches families directly. In cases tied to welfare programs like TANF, states can legally keep child support payments as "reimbursement," even though more than 70% of custodial parents receiving public aid live below the poverty line.

Meanwhile, the custodial parent is being monitored, evaluated, and penalized at every turn. Need housing? Prove your income. Need SNAP? Tell them who lives with you, how much do you pay in bills, do you have any assets, and how much you make down to the cent. But the parent who isn't contributing financially? No paperwork required. No forms. No urgency. And here's the hard truth: when support doesn't show up, the mother is the one subsidizing the father's portion. With the cost of raising a child averaging **$21,681 per year**, that means she's covering not only her half, about **$10,840,** but also his. Over 18 years, that adds up to more than

$195,000 per child that the absent parent should be contributing but isn't.

Let's be real, some of them would pay. They have paid. But the government takes the payment, especially in TANF-linked cases, and keeps it. And it is only passed through when fathers are not in arrears. They call it reimbursement, but it's really a handoff from one struggling parent to a system that still leaves the family behind. So now, both parents feel the weight. The one who stayed is overworked and underpaid. The one who left, or who was forced to give through garnishment has no access. No say, no power to help in other ways. And the child? They're still caught in the middle, asking for more than the system was ever built to give

Chapter 5

Who Really Benefits from the Brokenness?

Let's stop pretending this is just about missing money. This system, this illusion of support, it's not broken by accident. It's broken on purpose. And someone always benefits when a system is broken but still running.

Who profits when child support is unpaid but public aid keeps flowing? The state does. Nationwide, states collect billions annually in child support linked to welfare, and in 2022 alone, they retained over $1.38 billion that never reached families. That money doesn't go to the mother. It doesn't go to the child. It goes right back into state or federal hands as reimbursement. So, while politicians scream about cutting the

SNAP budget, they're out here keeping child support payments, never truly offering the parent monetary support.

Who profits when poor people are pushed into conflict, forced to go to court to get the bare minimum? Legal systems do. The family law industry generates more than $50 billion a year built on custody battles, enforcement hearings, and endless paperwork. They don't make money on peace. They make money on pain. And let's not forget the media. The ones pushing stories about "deadbeat dads" and "welfare queens." That narrative sells. It makes people comfortable. It keeps them distracted from asking real questions, like: Why is the child support enforcement system harsher on the parent who's barely surviving? Why isn't anyone demanding accountability from the ones who vanished?

The truth is that people benefit when we're too tired to fight back. When we're busy surviving. When we're isolated, shamed, or told it's our fault. That's what keeps the illusion alive. But the moment we start asking who's profiting, not just financially, but politically and socially from our struggle? That's when things start to shift.

Chapter 6

Worse Than an Unbeliever: What Scripture Really Says About Abandonment

There's a verse often quoted with conviction but rarely studied with compassion: *"But if anyone does not provide for his relatives, and especially for members of his household, he has denied the faith and is worse than an unbeliever."* That's 1 Timothy 5:8, and it tends to be tossed around like a moral hammer, usually at fathers. But what happens when we actually sit with the full context?

The chapter isn't just a rebuke to men. It's a reflection of an entire system. One that recognized how often women, especially widows and single mothers, were left without support. It outlines a communal ethic: that family should care for family, and when that's not possible, the community must step in. It was a call to preserve dignity and eliminate abandonment, not to shame individuals in isolation.

Today we've flipped the message. Instead of recognizing the spiritual weight of collective care, we point fingers at women who are struggling, and praise systems that punish rather than protect. If we truly believe in the Scripture, if we believe in what it means to *walk in faith*, then provision isn't just a paycheck. It's presence. It's effort. It's legacy.

That's what this book is about. Reclaiming not just fairness, but faithfulness. Not just accountability, but alignment. Because the truth is, if we all supported one another like Scripture says we should, the deficit wouldn't be just about dollars. It would be about how much love we've withheld from each other in the name of ego.

Chapter 7

Provision Isn't Always a Check—Sometimes It's a Circle

The truth is, I wouldn't have made it this far without community. There are some things that you must go through alone, but you don't have to go through everything alone. After my divorce, it was my family that helped me. They made up where I lacked. Sometimes with money, sometimes with time, sometimes just with a presence that reminded me that I wasn't alone. We all work together. We move like a circle. A symbiotic flow. That's what real provision looks like. But not everyone has that.

A lot of women are raising children in emotional and financial isolation, while the system that was supposed to help them has turned their struggle into a statistic or a stereotype. Instead of offering support, it polices them. Instead of asking why a father isn't present, it redirects the blame toward the mother for needing help at all. We were never supposed to carry this alone. The Bible didn't teach that. Nature didn't design that. Yet here we are, rewarding abandonment with silence and punishing survival with judgment.

Provision isn't just a check. It's the willingness to show up when someone else can't stand on their own. It's fathers being fathers. It's communities becoming safety nets. It's systems that protect without dehumanizing. And yet here we are, watching those same systems shout about "morality" while quietly stripping away dignity. They're putting prayer back in schools—but taking joy off the shelves for children whose parents receive SNAP. A mother buying her child a candy bar on the weekend shouldn't be a political statement. A family treating themselves to something sweet or buying snacks shouldn't be punished because they needed help to begin with.

They say it's about health, but there is a large portion of people who receive food stamps that don't have access to kitchens and ways to cook the food. There are many issues that need to be placed above restricting the smallest pleasures. Not because it's unhealthy, but because somewhere deep in the system, someone decided that poor families shouldn't be allowed joy. There are really people out here in the world that are jealous and angry with people who have less than them. The illusion of having help makes people resent those who need help the most.

No, the deficit isn't just financial. It's spiritual. It's structural. And it's a mirror of how far we've strayed from what true provision, true family, and true community were meant to be. We used to believe the system was just flawed.

Outdated, maybe. Underfunded. Just in need of a little fixing. But now? Now we see it for what it is. This is about missed payments and missed accountability. Not just about "absent fathers", but absent justice. And it's not just about policy, it's about power. About control. How people are positioned in a way that is just stable enough to function, but never free enough to rise.

They want people to accept this as normal. To carry the weight in silence. To pay the taxes quietly. To watch them hoard the resources for the wealthy. To shrink ourselves in shame while the system walks away clean, but with full pockets. We're done pretending. We're naming the imbalance. We're tracing the money. We're calling out the silence. And we're refusing to sit in the margins while they act like the full story's already been told.

Until we hold the entire system accountable, including the parts that profit from our pain, there will be no justice in child support. No dignity in the aid system. No equity in the courts. And as long as the illusion stands, the people who need the most will keep getting the least. But that illusion? It's cracking now. Because we see it. And once we see it, we can't unsee it. And once we name it, we can start to change it.

Chapter 8

Surviving the Gap

Nobody talks about the space in between. Not the court date. Not the judgment. Not the promise on paper. I'm talking about the gap. The space between when you should receive child support and when it actually comes... *if* it ever does. That's where the real story lives. That's where rent is due, but the payment didn't hit. Where shoes are needed, but you have to wait. Where the kids are sick, and you're wondering if you can afford the co-pay, let alone the gas to get there. Constant over the counter cold medicine. That's the part nobody sees, the mental, emotional, and physical toll of surviving the in-between. That stretch of time where you still have to show up like everything's handled, when inside, you're holding together a crumbling plan with prayer, hustle, and a second wind that you shouldn't have had to find.

Support is supposed to be a cushion. A bridge. A reliable presence. But for so many of us, it's a ghost. It's a maybe. It's a reminder that the system promised help, then went silent. That one salary is going to have to be enough. And still, we make it. We cook the meals. We delay bills. We work extra hours. We lean on community if we're lucky, or solitude if we're not. We do what it takes because our children need what the system won't deliver. But that gap? It changes you. It wears you down. And some days, just surviving it is the win.

Chapter 9

It's Not Part of the Plan

Imagine trying to build a financial plan around something that may or may not come. You can't. That's the thing about child support for some of us, it's not dependable, or it doesn't exist. It's not consistent enough to be part of the actual strategy. So no, it's not penciled in when I'm sitting down with my bills. It's not in the budget spreadsheet. It's not part of the rent money or the grocery list or the field trip envelope. And because of that, I don't wait on it. I can't.

There are moments when I'll send a text, "Can you send some money for the kids?" Because yes, sometimes I need that extra help. But I've learned not to expect it. When it does come, a Zelle here, a little generosity there, I'm grateful. I really am. But it's not something I bank on.

The bills don't pause because support didn't come through. The light company doesn't care about your co-parent's mood. And your kid's needs don't go away because the system is backed up. So, I always have to have another plan. Even if it's messy. Even if it's hard. Because the kids don't get to live in "maybe." They live in right now. And honestly, that's where the stress really lives. Not in waiting on child support, but in trying to stretch what you do have when everything keeps coming back to back: rent, food, school supplies, a birthday, a haircut, a doctor visit, a project due tomorrow. There's always another expense. That's the reality of surviving the gap. And nobody sees it unless they've lived it.

Chapter 10

The Strength They Don't See

What people don't realize is that this kind of survival builds something in you. Something deep. It builds a type of resilience that can't be faked. A strength you don't even know you have until you're out here holding everything down with nothing but willpower and love.

They see the mom at the bus stop, the woman checking her balance before the swipe, the parent juggling work and pickups and tired eyes, but they don't see the strength. The kind of strength it takes to keep going with no guaranteed help. To create peace in a house where chaos could've lived.

Yes, it would be nice to get a break. It feels unfair sometimes to be the one who does it all and still gets overlooked. But we know something deeper. We know that our soil is pure. That the love we pour into our children is clean, whole, unshaken. They're not growing up in tension. They're not watching us chase or beg. They're watching us rise.

It's a double-edged sword, sure. Sometimes you feel the sting of doing it alone. But on the other side of that sword? There's freedom. There's quiet. There's no drama in your doorway. No co-parent to argue with. No unpredictable storm to brace yourself against. And in that space, you realize you've created something sacred. Your kids are loved. Your home is steady. And that gap, that ache that once felt like lack, is now a testament to just how strong you really are.

Chapter 11

We Don't Just Survive the Gap—We Redefine It

They thought the gap would break us. That the silence, the missing support, the weight of doing it all would wear us down. But instead, we adapted. We got smarter. We got stronger. We learned how to make peace in the middle of the pressure. We learned how to raise kings and queens with limited means but unlimited love. We are going back to school. We are creating businesses. We are changing our mindsets, our careers, and leveling up our circumstances. So no, we don't just survive the gap.

We *run it.*

We *shape it.*

We *stretch it into a legacy.*

And if the system won't show up for us, then we'll build our own. Brick by brick. Day by day. Because we were never just waiting. We were becoming.

Chapter 12

The Cost of Showing Up

The cost of showing up isn't always counted in dollars.

It's counted in sacrifices. In sleepless nights. In the way your body aches but you still get up. It's in all the times you rearranged your life so your kids wouldn't have to feel what was missing. Because for some of us, showing up means being the only one. The only one clapping in the stands, the only one at the parent-teacher meeting, the only one packing lunches, checking homework, remembering birthdays, and wiping tears.

We do it, not because it's easy, but because we promised ourselves we would never let them feel that void. It means that no matter what's going on in your own life, your job, your health, your emotions, you don't get to disappear. You don't get to break down. You don't get to clock out. Showing up means you carry your life and theirs. It means handling school calls during work hours. It means dragging yourself out the bed on days when your body says no, because your child has a performance, or a dentist appointment, or just a rough morning and needs you there.

There are no days off from showing up. And most of the time? No one sees that part. No one claps for the person who's always there. They just expect it. But that presence? That daily, steady, reliable love? That's the part that changes everything.

Chapter 13

Still, We Go

Here's the truth: we're not always struggling. We're surviving. We're thriving. We're building. But we've all had those moments. The burnout moment. The crash moment. The moment where your body is moving but your spirit is over it. It's not every day. But it hits.

There are days we're just tired of being responsible. Tired of being the one everyone calls. Tired of holding the schedule, the rules, the energy. There are days we don't want to do the homework. We don't want to sit through practice. We don't want to play chauffeur, chef, therapist, and project manager back-to-back. We just want to sit. Sip iced coffee. Watch a show in silence. Breathe.

We don't get that luxury, not without earning it first. Not without negotiating it. Not without guilt sometimes creeping in. So even when we want to disappear for a minute, we show up anyway. Because they're watching. Because they need us. Because they deserve that version of us, even when we're tired. That's not weakness. That's power in motion. That's love without pause. And that's the cost. It's not the money. It's the constancy of it. The way you keep pouring, keep giving, keep standing, even when nobody claps, even when no one says thank you.

Chapter 14

Invisible Labor, Universal Impact

Society has a habit of undervaluing this kind of work.

They call it "just parenting," or "what you're supposed to do,"

like it doesn't require sacrifice. Like it doesn't hold entire

generations together. But the truth is, the labor of mothers,

especially those doing it alone, offers great value to this

country.

We are raising the next workforce, the next leaders,

the next teachers, builders, thinkers, protectors. We are also a

part of that. We are holding it down emotionally and

economically. We are managing trauma, breaking generational cycles, filling in the gaps left by systems that were never built with us in mind. And still, this labor is invisible.

We don't get overtime. We don't get paid leave. We don't get policy written with our names in mind. But without us, nothing moves. Nothing grows. Nothing heals. Every community's safety is tied to how stable its homes are. Every economy depends on the people we raise.
And every future depends on whether these children grow up with love, support, and someone who shows up for them, even when it's hard. At any moment you can become a single parent, whether through a traumatic event or through separation. So, the cost of showing up isn't just personal, it's national. It's cultural. It's global. And it's time we stop pretending this labor doesn't matter. Because it does.
It always has.

Chapter 15

A System Built to Reclaim, Not Support

Let's be real about where this all started. The Child Support Program wasn't created with the child in mind. It was designed to protect the government's pockets.

Beginning as a federal partnership, the goal wasn't to help struggling families. It was to reduce the cost of the Aid to Families with Dependent Children (AFDC) program. From 1935 to 1996, AFDC was one of the main sources of public assistance for families raising children alone. So, what did the system do? It started going after non-custodial parents, mostly fathers, to collect child support. But not to give that money to the kids. Oh no. That money went straight back to the state. It wasn't "child support." It was welfare reimbursement.

If the court ordered $100 in support, and that same family received $100 in AFDC, guess who got the payment? Not the child. Not the custodial parent. The state kept every dollar, and then split it with the federal government. That policy is still in effect today. Some states now "pass through" a portion of the payment to families, but many still keep most or all of it. And just like that, we see the truth: this system was never truly built for care. It was built for collection. Built for control. And it's been that way since the beginning.

Chapter 16

Debt by Design: How Child Support Became a Tool for State Reimbursement

When people hear "child support," they assume the money is going straight to the child. That has been the collective consensus and misunderstanding of how it works. But that's not how the system was built, and for too many families, that's still not how it works.

The Child Support Program wasn't born out of care or compassion for its American families. It was born out of budget protection. From 1935 through 1996, the federal Aid to Families with Dependent Children (AFDC) program helped provide a lifeline to families raising children with little or no support. But by the time the Child Support Program became formalized, its main goal wasn't about helping the child, it was about reimbursing the government for that public aid. That same model continues today.

In 2021 alone, the U.S. government kept $1.38 billion in collected child support payments. Not for the families. Not for the children. But for the state. All under the name of "cost recovery." This approach doesn't serve families, it taxes them. It treats child support like a debt owed to the government, not a right owed to the child. It punishes the poor for being poor and uses enforcement tools like wage garnishment, license suspension, and jail time to extract money from people who already have very little. And it does this without offering real solutions.

The real question is, how can we reimburse single mothers for back child support owed. How can we create laws that are fair to the citizens. The laws should be looking to act as a mediator, even if they have to intercept payments. Just because the father did not pay the child support voluntarily, doesn't mean that they should get to keep the check. And if the government gets reimbursed for state funded programs via child support, that should add to the budget. This is not child support. This is state debt collection, dressed up as justice.

Chapter 17

When Support Becomes Strain

This isn't just about money, it's about what this system does to families, to relationships, and to futures. When the government treats child support like a reimbursement plan, it places custodial and non-custodial parents on opposite sides of a financial battlefield. One is left raising a child with too little. The other is being squeezed for cash they may not even have. And neither one walks away with peace.

It creates resentment. Not because either parent hates their child, but because the system inserts pressure where there should be partnership. Instead of encouraging connection or shared responsibility, it pits survival against survival. And too often, love gets lost in the middle.

This model especially harms low-income parents. A father who's already struggling to find steady work or housing now has child support debt stacked against him with interest, penalties, and threats. And here's the kicker: the child he's being forced to pay for isn't even getting the money. The government is. So, what happens? Tension builds. Communication breaks. The child is caught in the crossfire. And two people who *should* be figuring out how to co-parent become adversaries in a system designed to keep them there.

Generational poverty doesn't just start with parenting; it starts with policy. It starts with systems that pretend to help but actually destabilize. It starts with debt dressed up as duty, and punishment sold as protection. This isn't about what's "owed." This is about what's taken, and who benefits when the taking never stops.

Chapter 18

We Need Restoration, Not Reimbursement

If we want to fix this, we have to shift the entire mindset.

Child support cannot be about debt collection. It can't be

about punishment, control, or payback. It has to be about

stability for the child, for the parent raising them, and for the

parent expected to help.

What would a restorative system look like? It would

pass through 100% of child support payments to the family no

middleman, no reimbursement, no cut for the state. It would

offer job training, mental health support, and housing stability

instead of punishing poverty. It would end interest stacking and lifetime arrears that haunt people for decades, especially if those debts never reach the child or the mother.

It would provide mediation and co-parenting support, not just legal threats, to help families communicate and collaborate when they can. It would start with the needs of the child, not the deficits of the budget. And it would treat support like what it really is: an investment, not a penalty. If we want to break cycles, we can't keep building systems that profit from keeping people stuck. We need policies that free people up to show up, not just financially, but emotionally, spiritually, and fully.

Our kids deserve more than a broken pipeline of payments and promises. They deserve a system that restores what was lost... not one that takes even more.

We Need Restoration—*and* Repayment

Let's be clear: restoration doesn't mean letting go of what's owed. It means delivering what was promised, fully, fairly, and without delay. Child support should never be about state profit. It should be about the actual support of children, and the households holding them down. We want systems that work, yes. We want services, training, mental health care, and co-parenting support, yes. But let's not get it twisted, we want the money, too.

Every missed payment.
Every garnishment that never reached the family.
Every dollar the state held hostage in the name of "cost recovery."
Run. It. Back!!

We're not begging. We're demanding what's already been earned through sacrifice, through labor, through sleepless nights and showing up anyway. Restoration without repayment is just another lie wrapped in sympathy. We want

justice, and justice pays what it owes.

Chapter 19

Outside the System, Inside the Village

When the support didn't come, we didn't collapse, we got creative. We built carpools. We shared meals. We watched each other's kids. We handed down clothes, swapped stories, sent encouragement, and showed up in ways the system never could. And not because we had extra, but because we knew we couldn't survive in isolation.

While policies ignored us, and the courts made us wait, and the benefits fell short, our people didn't. The village didn't always look perfect. Sometimes it was a friend. Sometimes it was a cousin. Sometimes it was a teacher who looked out, a family member who slipped you something on the side, a friend who picked up your child when you were still at work. That kind of support is sacred. It's quiet. And it's powerful. It's not just about money, it's about presence. It's about reminding each other: you're not doing this alone.

Chapter 20

The Village Evolves

Today's village doesn't always look like the one our grandparents knew. It's not always on the same block or even in the same city. Sometimes it's in a group chat with people who remind you to breathe. Sometimes it's a neighbor who leaves food at your door. Sometimes it's a mama you met at daycare who becomes your emergency contact without question.

We've made digital villages. Late-night phone calls. Ride shares. "You got your lights paid?" check-ins. Care circles that come through when the system doesn't. It's not organized by the government. It's not sponsored. It's not formal. But it's real, and it's kept so many of us afloat. That's the kind of support no law can replace. And it's why, even when the child support check doesn't come, or the program gets denied, or the court hearing gets pushed back, we're still standing. Because the village holds.

Chapter 21

The Village We're Building

This generation doesn't always have the village we were told would be there. Some of us didn't grow up with extended family nearby. Some of us had family, but not the kind that shows up. And a lot of the traditional support systems like grandparents, aunties, strong neighborhood ties just aren't what they used to be. So, we've had to rebuild.

Our villages don't always come from blood; they come from bonds. From chosen family. From people who saw us struggling and stepped in, not out of obligation, but out of heart. It's the co-worker who covers your shift. The other mom at daycare who becomes your lifeline. The friend who sends you grocery money before you even ask. The teacher who stays late so your kid doesn't feel left out.

We are building our own networks in real time. Some of us are the first generation to be the village we never had. And it's hard sometimes, having to create what should've already been there. But it's powerful too. Because it means this time, it's being built with intention. With love. With survival and soul stitched into every connection.

Chapter 22

The Village We Keep, and the Village We Create

I'm blessed to have a village. It's not huge, but it's solid. My parents. My sister. An auntie and her family who shows up without me having to ask. It's a tight circle, but it's mine. And having that kind of support, the kind that doesn't come with judgment or conditions, is something that I don't take for granted. It's part of the reason I've been able to keep going when things got heavy. But I also know that's not everybody's story.

I've seen so many people piece together their support system from coworkers, friends, support groups, neighbors, or mentors. People who step up even when they're not blood. People who become aunties, uncles, big cousins, and safe spaces just by showing love. And sometimes, that's what the new village looks like. Some of us were born into it. Some of us built it. And some of us are becoming it for our kids, our friends, and the next mama who needs a hand.

Whether it's family you've known your whole life or someone you met two months ago who shows up like they've known you forever, that kind of support is everything. It's what holds us together when systems fall apart. Because when you have a village, even a small one, you're never doing this alone.

Chapter 23

Building Forward: The Legacy of the Village

The village isn't just about support, it's about legacy. It's about what we pass down. The values. The presence. The proof that love can be consistent even when life isn't. That somebody will show up, even when everything else says you're on your own.

Our kids are watching how we care for one another. They're watching how we lean on our parents, how we ask our friends for help, how we show up at graduations, birthday parties, hard days, and in-between moments. They're learning what it means to belong, and what it looks like to never give up on each other. And so, we pass it on.

We pass on the strength of family. The beauty of friendship. The unspoken rule that if I got it, you got it. That's the legacy of the village. Even if the system never recognizes its power, we know better. We've seen what it can do. Because while policies shift, and benefits get cut, and support systems rise and fall, the village endures. And if we protect it, nurture it, and expand it, it will outlive all of us.

Chapter 24

Welfare Queens, Deadbeat Dads, and Other Lies We've Been Told

These labels didn't come from the people living the story.

They came from the people watching it from a distance.

From politicians, media personalities, podcasters, and systems

that needed a scapegoat to justify policies that hurt the poor.

They told us single mothers were milking the system. But

billionaires get the bulk of government funding in government

contracts, loans, subsidies, and tax credits.

They told us that Black fathers had disappeared. But

according to the CDC 58% of Black fathers live with one or

more of their children. Even a larger majority 72.7% of Black fathers talk with their children about things that happened during the day. They speak with their children several times weekly or more often, whether they do or do not live with their children.

They told us that mothers were lazy and manipulative. That fathers were irresponsible and disposable, but why would we truly believe that. For too long, the world believed it. But here's the truth: those labels were never about truth, they were about control. About shaping a narrative that made it easier to cut benefits, criminalize poverty, and ignore the root causes of economic injustice. Because it's easier to blame the mother than to fix a broken system. It's easier to shame the father than to address systemic racism and generational trauma. It's easier to create a villain than to admit the policies have failed us. These myths have been weaponized, not just against individuals, but against entire families. And we're here to name them. Break them. Bury them.

Chapter 25

The Myth of the "Welfare Queen"

This one started as a political punchline, and it hit Black women the hardest. The so-called "welfare queen" was painted as a lazy, manipulative woman with too many kids and too much free time. Politicians used her as a symbol of government waste, someone gaming the system while "good taxpayers" footed the bill. But this woman? She never really existed. She was built in soundbites, not statistics. The real numbers tell a different story.

Most people on public assistance are working or actively seeking work. A portion are single mothers doing everything in their power to hold their households together.

And let's be honest: nobody's living large on food stamps. Nobody's getting rich from Section 8. These programs barely cover survival. There is no luxury in needing help. But the myth served a purpose. It made people comfortable slashing benefits. It fueled public judgment. It gave the illusion that poverty was a choice, and that help was being abused.

In reality, the women raising kids while working jobs that don't pay enough, while going to school, while fighting to stay afloat? Those women are the backbone of this country, not a burden to it. We all pay taxes. We pay taxes on everything over and over and over again. The government is going to take your money anyways. Wouldn't you rather your money help people that need it, than going to a rich billionaire? I think that is the real perspective that we should be looking at.

Chapter 26

The Myth of the "Deadbeat Dad"

The term "deadbeat dad" gets used like it's the full story. But it's not. It's only a piece of a much bigger picture. Yes, some men walk away. They vanish. They leave one parent holding it all and barely look back. And yes, there are fathers who can pay and simply choose not to. There are a lot of them. That's real. That's painful. And that's a choice that leaves emotional and financial damage behind. But not every absent parent is acting out of malice.

Some are struggling. Some are navigating broken systems that make it hard to catch up once they fall behind. When their license gets suspended, it's harder to get to work.

When warrants stack up, they can't move freely. Some end up hiding, not because they don't care, but because they don't know how to come back without being penalized all over again. It doesn't excuse the absence. It doesn't remove accountability. But it does complicate the label.

Not every man trying to hold onto his check is doing it out of cruelty. Sometimes it's fear. Sometimes it's pride. Sometimes it's just survival. And sometimes, yes, it's selfishness. Flat out. But until we start separating the struggle from the spite, and the pain from the patterns, we'll keep lumping everyone together under the same tired label. No one wins from that, especially not the child.

Chapter 27

The Cost of Believing the Lie

These myths haven't just shaped opinions, they've shaped lives. They've divided families. Turned co-parents into enemies. It made people believe that if a mom needed help, she must be lazy. That if a dad fell behind, he must be worthless. That one parent is always the villain, and the other is always the victim. But life is more complex than that. And people are more layered than the media ever gives them credit for.

These narratives have crept into our conversations, our group chats, our memes, our podcasts. They've become gospel in places where no one's bothering to check the facts. And once you believe the lie long enough, it becomes hard to imagine anything else. It's easier to laugh at a stereotype than to challenge it. It's easier to blame than to understand. It's easier to repost than to research.

We sit in cycles of shame, of silence, of broken trust, thinking that this is just how it is. But it's not. Because underneath the noise, there are parents trying. There are families trying to heal. There are mothers who work and raise children with no praise. Fathers who are climbing out of debt just to stay in their child's life. Grandparents stepping in. Communities holding each other down. And those stories don't go viral. But they're real. And they deserve to be heard.

Chapter 28

A Single Parent Budget: A month in Numbers

A single parent household often operates with one income stretched to cover the needs of two or more people. I'm going to turn the invisible math into visible numbers. If we use baseline assumptions, the average monthly income for a single parent is "$3200". I personally have two children. An expense breakdown could look like this:

Expenses Breakdown (example ranges)

- **Housing & Utilities**: Rent/mortgage, lights, water, internet ($1,200–$1,600).

- **Food**: Groceries, school lunches, snacks ($500–$800).

- **Childcare/Education**: Daycare, after-school, supplies ($600–$1,000).

- **Transportation**: Gas, insurance, car payment or public transit (~$400–$700).

- **Healthcare**: Insurance premiums, co-pays, prescriptions ($300–$500).

- **Clothing & Essentials**: Kids grow fast—shoes, seasonal clothes ($100–$200).

- **Debt/Loans/Credit**: Student loans, credit card minimums ($200–$400).

- **Miscellaneous**: Birthdays, school trips, emergencies ($150–$250).

That is a $3450- $5450 price range on bills. This doesn't include child support. This is why some of the child support payment goes to the mother as well as the child. Why picking apart how the mother spends the child support payments is a selfish viewpoint. When a man skips a payment, they don't care that the mother is paying that portion, but it is a large portion to cover. And let me be clear, the numbers look like that for everyone. But its time for balance and an equal distribution of financial responsibility.

Chapter 29

Reclaiming the Narrative

It's time to rewrite the story.

No more letting media tell us who we are.

No more accepting policy shaped by stereotypes.

No more sitting in silence while families are torn apart by assumptions and soundbites.

We are more than the labels.

We are more than the lies.

We are not "welfare queens."

We are not "deadbeat dads."

We are survivors. Builders. Providers. Protectors. Nurturers.

We are the foundation.

And now we take the narrative back.

We speak the truth in courtrooms, classrooms, and community centers.

We hold each other accountable with compassion and clarity, not shame.

We demand policies that see us fully, and systems that serve us justly.

We refuse to let our children grow up in the shadow of stereotypes.

This isn't just about calling out a myth. It's about changing the culture.

So let this be the beginning.

Of healing.

Of reunion.

Of unity.

Of policy built on truth, not fear.

Let this be the moment we reclaim the story for our families,

our future, and ourselves.

Chapter 30

And One More Thing: It's Okay

Let's say this too, loud and clear: It is okay for relationships to end. It is okay for people to realize they weren't meant to last forever. It is okay for a couple to fall apart and still rise as co-parents. The failure of a relationship does not mean the failure of a family.

We've got to stop attaching shame to the words baby mama and baby daddy, like they cancel out our worth. We've got to stop talking about single parents like they're broken, or like they messed up. Because what's broken is the idea that love only counts if it lasts forever. That partnership only matters if it fits into a neat little box.

The truth is that our children are still here. And they still need love, structure, stability, and support. So even if the romance is over, the family remains. Even if the relationship didn't survive, the responsibility does. And that's okay. Being a family isn't about matching last names or sharing a roof. It's about showing up, doing the work, and putting the child first. Once we start honoring that truth, we'll stop the shame. And we'll start building something real.

Chapter 31

Co-Parenting in Name Only

They call it co-parenting. But for some of us, it's a label with no weight. No action behind it. No shared effort. Just a title thrown around to make it sound like the work is being split when it's really falling on one person. People say, "Well at least you're co-parenting," like it's a compliment.

The truth is, a lot of us are doing 90% of the work while someone else gets credit for a presence they don't actually provide. Co-parenting isn't just having your name on the birth certificate. It's not a monthly phone call. It's not dropping by when it's convenient. It's the every day. The emotional, physical, spiritual presence. It's being there even when it's hard, inconvenient, or uncomfortable. And when one parent is doing it all, the other just shows up for the highlight reel. That's not co-parenting. That's performance.

Chapter 32

You Can't Just Show Up for the Spotlight

To the fathers who only come around for the fun moments,
the birthdays, the trophies, the Christmas photos, this is your
wake-up call. Being a parent is not a highlight reel. It's the
quiet, unseen, sometimes uncomfortable labor of love that
happens every single day. It's wiping noses, calming tantrums,
helping with homework, being there when your child is
frustrated, unsure, or afraid. That's where trust is built. That's
where character is shaped.

Showing up just for the victories isn't enough.
Showing up only when your child is in the spotlight isn't
enough. They don't just need you in the stands when they're

winning, they need you on the sidelines when they're struggling. They need your presence to be consistent, not convenient. Because the truth is, these kids don't raise themselves. They are being poured into daily by women who are exhausted, resilient, stretched thin, and still giving everything they have.

We don't just want help, we want partnership. We want grounded, emotionally present, spiritually awakened men leading their children, not just entertaining them. This is a call to be more. To step into the role God gave you, not just biologically, but spiritually. Because if you've ever imagined yourself as a king, as a creator, as someone made in the image of God, then hear this:

Parenting is the closest you will ever come to understanding that power.

To create life.

To nurture it.

To guide it.

To comfort it.

To protect it.

To teach it right from wrong and pour love into a soul until it knows it's safe.

That is divine work.

And when you avoid it, you're not just missing moments, you're missing your purpose.

Chapter 33

What True Co-Parenting Could Be

Co-parenting isn't about being perfect. It's about being present consistently, honestly, and with intention. It's not just about splitting weekends or picking up gifts on birthdays. It's about making sure your child knows you are emotionally available, spiritually grounded, and willing to share the real weight of parenting.

True co-parenting looks like communication. It looks like showing up even when it's awkward. It looks like being proactive, not reactive, checking in, offering help, participating in decisions, not just reacting to crises or celebrations. It looks like holding space for the mother of your child even if the relationship didn't work out, because peace in the parenting dynamic benefits the child first. It looks like respect. It looks like maturity. It looks like healing. And most of all? It looks like putting ego down, and love first.

Chapter 34

For the Ones Who Want to Do Better

To the fathers who want to show up but don't know how: this is for you too. Maybe you were never taught how to be emotionally present. Maybe your father was absent. Maybe life has been heavy and messy, and you've stayed distant because you thought your child didn't need you, or because you didn't know how to face what's been lost.

Let me tell you something: It's not too late. Children remember who shows up. And even if they're older now, even if things have been rough, it matters that you try. It matters that you're consistent. And it matters that you own your part. In some cases, there is room for redemption in parenting.

There is room for reconnection. But it starts with humility, honesty, and the willingness to step in without fanfare. Your child doesn't need perfection. They need you to be real. They need you to try. And the moment you decide to lead from love instead of guilt or pride, you've already taken the first step.

Chapter 35

A Vision for Healing

As a Black woman, this isn't just about parenting, it's about restoration. It's about rising again as a community. It's about repairing what history tried to tear apart, our families, our love, our unity. I want to see healing between children and their parents, all their parents. Mothers and fathers. Biological and chosen. Those who've been there, and those who are just now realizing they need to step up.

I know not every relationship can be mended. I know some wounds run deep. But where healing is possible, we should fight for it. Because our children deserve homes that are whole, not perfect, but peaceful. And if you can't be emotionally available, you can still be financially accountable. You can still contribute. You can still show support. You can still choose not to bring chaos into the space your child is trying to grow in. That choice matters.

I see a future where the Black community is not just surviving but thriving. Where our families are led by love, not ego. Where fathers are present. Where mothers are supported. Where children are free to rise because the village is rooted again. We are not broken, we are healing. And every step we take toward showing up for our children is a step back toward our power.

Chapter 36

Where's the Reform?

We've named the problem. We've felt the pain. We've broken down the lies, exposed the systems, told the truth behind the labels. Now it's time to ask the question that echoes through every chapter of this book: Where is the reform? Because we're tired of surviving broken systems. Tired of watching politicians debate numbers while children go without. Tired of parents, especially mothers, being stretched to the edge while the government keeps the money and pushes the blame.

We don't need more speeches. We need change. Real reform means we stop chasing symptoms and start addressing root causes. It means shifting child support from punishment to partnership. It means policies that treat parents like people, not paychecks. It means systems that are built around children's needs, not state reimbursement.

Chapter 37

What Real Reform Could Look Like

We don't need tweaks, we need a full reset.

1. Pass Through 100% of Child Support Payments

If support is collected, it should go to the child. Not the state. Not as reimbursement. Not through back-end deals. Every dollar belongs to the family it was meant for.

2. End Interest and Lifetime Arrears on Poverty-Based Debt

Parents shouldn't be crushed by interest on payments they

couldn't afford in the first place. If a parent is low-income or receiving aid, the system should pause, not punish.

3. Invest in Job Training and Economic Opportunities

Enforcement isn't the only answer. If we want families to thrive, we need job support for non-custodial parents. Give them tools to succeed, not just threats of jail or license suspension.

4. Redesign Co-Parenting Support Services

Offer mediation, education, and emotional wellness programs, not just courtrooms. Help parents work together even when the relationship is over. Free and affordable family therapy. Because the child deserves that peace.

5. Shift the Narrative at Every Level

End the stigma around single parents, especially Black mothers. Stop recycling myths that shame families and ignore systemic injustice. Build policies based on data and lived experience, not stereotypes.

6. Hold Systems Accountable, Not Just Parents

Stop allowing the government to deflect problems onto the people, and hold them accountable for implementing policies that can help balance out the financial child support deficit. Let's get these women paid and create more stability.

What We Really Want Is Dignity

This is bigger than money.

It's about *dignity*.

It's about *justice*.

It's about giving families space to thrive, not just survive.

We want policies that see the full story. That understand the emotional labor of caregiving. That honor the efforts of parents, especially the ones who never left. That offer support, not surveillance. We want our kids to see us fighting for more, not just for ourselves, but for them.

To grow up in a world where support is expected, not begged for. Where showing up isn't optional. Where love and leadership go hand in hand.

This is the movement. This is the moment. We are not just raising children, we are raising the next generation of culture-shapers, nation-builders, and cycle-breakers. And they deserve systems that match the power we're pouring into them. So, when we ask, "Where's the reform?" we're not asking quietly. We're demanding answers. And we're building the future in the meantime.

Chapter 38

Invisible Resilience

There's a kind of strength the world praises, especially in mothers, particularly Black mothers, that looks like power on the outside but feels like pressure on the inside. You hear it in phrases like "she always holds it down" or "you're so strong, I don't know how you do it." But what they don't say is, "How can I help you?" or "Are you okay?" I didn't ask to be resilient. I became resilient because I had no choice. I didn't get to collapse. I didn't get to pass the baton. I had to figure it out emotionally, financially, and spiritually on days when even getting out of bed felt like a task.

The truth is that resilience is a badge of honor. It's not something we chose but it's something God gave us. It helps keep us going when everything said stop. That kind of strength is sacred. But being called "strong," or labeled a "single independent Black woman," isn't the same as being supported. Those phrases sound empowering on the surface, but they're often used to excuse why help never shows up.

We don't wear independence like an accessory, we carry it like armor because we have no choice. That doesn't mean we don't want help. We just got tired of waiting on it. And yet, the world rewards that silence. We're told to "keep it together," "don't be bitter," and "make it look easy." But making it look easy robs us of the help we deserve.

This chapter isn't about complaining. It's about naming what has been unspoken for too long. Because when you name it, you can change it. You can say, "I'm tired," and still be a good mother. You can say, "I need help," and still be strong. You can choose softness without losing power. Invisible resilience doesn't mean we're broken. It means we've been carrying more than anyone sees. But we don't have to carry it alone anymore. We have the freedom to choose. We have the freedom to change.

Chapter 39

The Price of Peace

That kind of resilience comes with a cost. When you're truly focused on your kids and being present, protective, and intentional, there are things you give up that no one sees. You don't just sacrifice rest or money. You sacrifice relationships. You stop dating because if you do, people assume your new partner is paying your bills or parenting your children. As a mother you have an obligation to protect your children from predators and a revolving door of failed relationships. You stop letting new people in because every connection is treated like a threat to your priorities.

The world doesn't just expect you to be strong. It expects you to be alone in your strength. If you find time to love, they'll say you're neglecting your kids. If you make space for yourself, they'll say you're selfish. So many mothers choose solitude, not because they want it, but because judgment is louder than grace.

The world doesn't just expect you to be strong. It expects you to be alone in your strength. Some mothers feel trapped by that judgment. Worried about being seen as a "bad mom" or having their choices used against them. And yes, perception can matter, especially when you're trying to protect your children from gossip, false claims, or even systems that are quick to punish.

Honestly, I'm not moved by judgment. I don't shape my life around what people think of me. That's not my burden. What I care about is raising my children well, and protecting our peace. But even with that strength, I see how many mothers' sacrifice connection. They sacrifice friendships, romance, even sisterhood, just to avoid the extra noise. And that isolation? That's the part that hurts.

I'm not closed off to love. I'm just not willing to abandon myself to have it. If it comes, it has to come with peace, not pressure. Respect, not rescue. Because I've done too much work to settle for anything that drains me. I don't just want love, I need partnership.

Chapter 40

Labor That Powers the World but Pays Nothing

There's a kind of work that doesn't come with a paycheck or a title. No applause. No "Employee of the Month" parking space. But it never stops. For single mothers, this labor is constant, packing lunches at dawn, juggling appointments, cleaning up messes both seen and unseen. It's not just physical work; it's the mental load of remembering every school deadline, every doctor visit, every bill due. It's waking up tired and going to bed exhausted, still wondering if you did enough.

This isn't a shared responsibility. It is a system powered by one dedicated individual. This invisible labor powers households, stabilizes children's lives, and fills in the cracks where policy fails. And yet, it remains unseen in the systems that measure productivity and value.

Globally, the value of unpaid labor mostly done by women, has been estimated at over ten trillion dollars a year. That's more than the combined worth of the world's biggest tech companies. But none of that shows up on a paycheck. For single mothers, it's even more intense. They're often performing multiple jobs at once: caregiver, provider, therapist, teacher, and logistical coordinator, all without compensation. If the hours spent on caregiving, housework, and mental planning were counted like paid labor, many single mothers would be logging overtime every single week.

It's not just time, it's energy. The kind that doesn't refill with a nap or a day off, because there usually isn't a day off. Every decision, what to cook, how to stretch the grocery budget, whether to stay home with a sick child or risk losing a day's pay all takes mental energy. It's a full-time calculation on how to survive, stretch, and sustain. And when you're the only adult in the house, there's no passing the baton. That constant state of alertness, hyper-managing every detail, adds up to burnout, not balance.

This hidden labor doesn't just wear you down, it boxes you in. The hours spent managing home life often mean fewer hours available for paid work, let alone career advancement. Many single mothers are forced to choose jobs based on flexibility, not growth. Jobs that allow for school drop-offs, sick days, and surprise emergencies, but rarely offer benefits, stability, or promotions. And even when they do work full-time, the "motherhood penalty" still applies. Studies show that each young child can reduce a mother's earnings by up to fifteen percent. When no one else is there to absorb the shocks. Financial, emotional, or logistical, single mothers are left to carry it all and pay the cost in lost income and opportunity.

According to Oxfam, if women were paid just the minimum wage for the unpaid care work they do, it would add up to over ten point eight trillion dollars globally each year. In the U.S. alone, single mothers contribute hundreds of billions in invisible labor work that sustains families, communities, and even economies, yet remains uncompensated. And while this labor keeps society running, the women behind it are often running on empty.

It's one thing to measure time and wages, but the toll of hidden labor goes deeper than dollars. It seeps into the body, the mind, the spirit. So next, we'll break it down, not just what single mothers do, but what it costs them in rest, in relationships, in their own sense of self.

Mental health often takes the first hit when you're carrying invisible labor alone. Anxiety becomes a constant companion, worrying about money, about safety, about whether your kids feel secure. Depression creeps in quietly, disguised as exhaustion, numbness, or the feeling that you're just going through the motions. And with limited time, limited access to therapy, and sometimes even stigma within your own community, care for yourself falls to the bottom of the list. If it's on the list at all. For many single mothers, survival mode becomes a lifestyle, not a phase.

The hidden labor of single mothers isn't just a personal struggle, it's a societal blind spot. It's work that holds up entire communities. Yet, it remains invisible in the systems meant to support families. To see it, to name it, is the first step toward valuing it. But real change means more than awareness. It means restructuring how we measure work, support caregivers, and invest in those who give the most and receive the least. Until then, single mothers will continue doing the job of many, quietly, powerfully, and too often, alone.

Chapter 41

Debt By Design

So many single mothers aren't asking for punishment, they're asking for partnership. For stability. For a father to just show up in some way, even if it's not a perfect amount. But what ends up happening is that once the system kicks in, it turns into something cold and calculated. If a payment is missed, fees stack up. If someone can't pay, their license gets suspended. Then they can't get to work. Then they fall further behind.

What was meant to help the child becomes a spiral of shame and debt, mostly affecting Black and brown fathers who already face barriers to stable employment. And while all this is happening guess who's still covering the rent, the groceries, the school clothes? Mama.

You're not bitter, you're responsible. And you're doing what you have to do to keep the household going. But the way this system is structured in the life of a single parent? It doesn't support the parents doing the work or the one trying to catch up. It just piles on more weight.

I didn't put my children's father on child support to be bitter. I didn't do it out of spite, revenge, or anger. I did it because I needed help, and I still do. Raising children isn't free, and it isn't easy. I would be happy just to receive what the court ordered. Not more. Not some dream amount. Just the basics. Just consistency. Because it's not about it, it's about our children. It's about having enough to keep the lights on, to take them out to eat, instead of cooking all the meals. It's about lifting some of the weight off of my shoulders long enough for me to take a quick break. It's about not having to choose between school snacks and gas. But what people don't understand is how quickly the system stops working for anybody when a payment is missed.

When a payment is missed, it doesn't just disappear, it multiplies. Most states charge interest on unpaid child support, and it adds up fast. Some rates go as high as ten or twelve percent. Miss a few months, and suddenly what started as a few hundred dollars turns into thousands in arrears. And once you fall behind, it's like trying to climb out of a pit with no ladder. Wages get garnished. Tax refunds get seized. Passports get denied. Licenses get suspended, and that usually ends in traffic tickets and warrants. Because now, you can't legally drive to work to make the money they say you owe. It's a form of entrapment that not every man deserves to deal with.

This system wasn't built for grace. It was built to run and collect. And when it comes to arrears, the unpaid support that stacks up, it doesn't care whether a parent is trying. It doesn't really matter why someone fell behind. The debt keeps growing. According to federal reports, over $115 billion in unpaid child support is owed in the U.S., and most of it will never be collected.

In fact, a study from the Urban Institute found that in states with high arrears balances, a significant portion of the debt is owed by parents who have no reported income at all. Yet the penalties keep coming, often landing hardest on Black fathers and low-income men. Those already locked out of economic opportunity. This isn't child support. It's a cycle of debt that benefits the state more than the family.

While the debt piles up on their end, the pressure piles up on mine. Because no matter what the court says, no matter what the balance sheet shows, I'm still the one making it happen. The one who has to figure it out when support doesn't come through. The one who stretches the groceries, finds a way to pay the light bill, and shows up at parent-teacher conferences like everything's fine. There's no arrears account for the unpaid hours I give every day. With no interest collecting on the emotional labor I invest. And yet, I'm expected to keep going like I'm not owed anything.

This isn't just about policy, it's about equity. If the system really cared about children, it would stop making it harder for both parents to show up. It would stop turning missed payments into numbers on a spreadsheet and broken systems into profit centers. And it would finally ask a better question: not just "Who owes what?" but "What does this child truly need, and how do we get there together?"

Until we stop treating support like a debt to punish, and start seeing it as a responsibility to share, we will keep failing the very people we claim to protect. The children and the parents doing everything they can to hold it all together.

Chapter 42

The Emotional Math of Motherhood

Some people think raising a child is just about having enough money. But honestly, the real currency that I'm always running out of is energy and time. Before I even walk into the grocery store, I've already done a full mental shift into project manager mode. I have to sit down, check my accounts, map out the week, estimate bills, and figure out what I can squeeze in without overdrafting. That's before I even think about food or anything extra.

The emotional math is exhausting. It's not just about "Can I afford this?" It's, "Will I have enough gas to make it to work and back all week?" "If I pay this light bill today, will we have enough to get my oil changed next week?" And it's a constant loop in my head because there's no real cushion. No backup. No partner checking in to say, "I've got it this time."

The real cost of raising a child today isn't just financial. It's mental. It's emotional. And for single parents, it feels like we're constantly budgeting parts of ourselves just to make it all fit. Sometimes, the hardest decisions are the ones nobody else even notices. Like standing in the kitchen after a long day, staring at a pile of dishes and thinking, "Should I just grab some takeout and save myself the stress?" But then that other voice hits: "If I spend that fifty dollars now, I might be short later in the week." So, I choose the dishes. I choose the grind. I choose exhaustion, because that's the cheaper option.

It's like that every day. Every little decision feels heavy because there's no margin. It's not just about saving money, it's about protecting my peace, conserving my energy, and avoiding burnout. But the cost is me. My body. My sleep. My ability to show up tomorrow feeling whole.

Raising a child in today's economy doesn't leave space for softness. It demands strategy, sacrifice, and stamina. And when you're doing it alone, every choice feels like it's holding up the entire house. But even in the middle of all that, my kids keep me grounded. They keep life interesting. There are days I don't want to be responsible, don't want to calculate or cook or stretch one more dollar. But then I hear them laughing in the other room, or I get one of those random hugs for no reason, and suddenly the weight shifts. Doesn't disappear. But it shifts.

It's not that I hate being a parent. I love my children deeply. I just hate how hard the world makes it to raise them in peace. I hate that doing the right things, showing up, providing, staying strong sometimes feels like I'm running on fumes with no pit stop in sight. But, being a single parent isn't all gloom. There's beauty in it. There's pride. There are dance parties in the kitchen and silly stories at bedtime. But there's also a cost. And too often, we're paying it in silence.

Still, through it all, I have peace. God has given me that. I may not always have the money I want, or the time I wish for, but I do have peace. Because I know I'm doing right by my children. I'm showing up. I'm providing. I'm choosing love, stability, and presence every single day.

Every mother has her own battle to fight, her own villain to face. But there's a different kind of rest that comes when you know you didn't quit. I don't carry the guilt of abandoning my kids. I sleep with the peace of knowing they're safe, they're loved, and I'm doing the best I can. That's not failure. That's victory, daily.

We might feel a little mom guilt when we take time for ourselves, sure. But deep down, we know we're handling business. We're raising the next generation with everything we've got, and doing it with strength, grace, and faith. That's not just survival. That's legacy.

Chapter 43

Legacy in Real Time

There's something powerful about choosing to break cycles. To wake up every day and say, "It ends with me." That's what parenting has become for so many of us, it's not just about survival, but about shifting the legacy. About passing down more than struggle. About rewriting the blueprint.

I think about DNA sometimes, not just the biological kind, but the spiritual kind. The legacy encoded in our choices, in how we show love, discipline, teach, and protect. We're not just raising kids. We're imprinting futures. And for single mothers especially, there's a sacred kind of fire in that.

Because we're doing it without the full village. Without the full funding. But we're still doing it with full hearts.

I don't just want my children to remember how hard I worked; I want them to remember how deeply I believed in them. How I spoke life over them even when I was tired. How I chose patience when the world pushed me to be harsh. That's legacy. Not just surviving, but modeling strength without bitterness. Power without pride. Grace without apology.

I want them to know that our circumstances didn't define us. That yes, we came through struggle, but we didn't let it break us. We used it as a tool. We used it to build discipline, faith, and creativity. That's what gets passed down. That's the kind of DNA I want echoing through generations. I always speak life over my children. I pray over them. I tell them that their minds are like computers. If something isn't working, you can reset it. Recode it. Reprogram your thoughts, and you can shift your whole reality. I want them to believe that no dream is too far if they're willing to do the inner work.

Everything I teach them, I've had to learn myself. Motherhood didn't just make me a parent, it made me a student. It taught me that you have to work hard yes, but you also have to work smart, work healed, and work with vision. It's not just about making it through the day. It's about building a life they'll one day be proud to inherit.

They're always watching. Even when I think they're distracted or too young to understand, they're paying attention. To how I move. To how I speak. To how I recover when life hits hard. They see me get up on the days I don't feel like it. They hear me praying in the kitchen, talking to God like He's sitting right beside me. They feel it when I choose not to snap, even though I'm exhausted. And all of that is becoming part of their code. That's the legacy I'm leaving. Not just the words I say, but the energy I carry. The example I set.

Every time I show up with love, with intention, with faith, I'm rewriting the blueprint. I'm handing them something better. Something rooted in truth, not trauma.

I'm not just raising my children, I'm breaking patterns that go back generations. I'm healing in real time. There are things I had to learn the hard way, things no one prepared me for. But I decided it ends with me. The silence. The struggle behind closed doors. The self-sacrifice that leaves nothing left for yourself. I'm rewriting that story.

I show my kids what it looks like to rest, to say no, to set boundaries and still be kind. I show them that love isn't just what you give to others, it's what you give to yourself. I'm teaching them not just how to survive this world, but how to walk through it whole.

Here's the thing, they inspire me just as much as I pour into them. Their questions stretch me. Their laughter lifts me. Their resilience reminds me of my own. Watching them grow, seeing the way they trust me and love me, it's a mirror. And every day, they remind me why this legacy matters.

I see a future for my children that's full of freedom. The freedom to choose their path without fear, freedom to express who they are without apology, freedom to thrive without carrying the weight of unhealed wounds. I see them walking into rooms with confidence, knowing they belong there. I see them building families, businesses, dreams with a foundation rooted in love, not lack.

I know that future isn't just wishful thinking. It's the result of what I'm doing now. Every late night, every prayer, every moment I hold it together when I'd rather fall apart, that's seed work. I'm sowing into their self-worth. Into their emotional safety. Into their spiritual depth. Into their vision of what's possible.

My legacy isn't just what I leave behind when I'm gone, it's what I'm building right now, in every hug, every lesson, every sacrifice. And when I see my kids smile, when I hear them repeat back the affirmations I whispered into their mornings, I know, I'm already watching the harvest begin.

Chapter 44

Carrying it All Every Day

The stress of being a single parent is always there. Whether things are calm or chaotic, whether the bills are paid now or at the last minute, it's there. That invisible strain. That pressure that lives in your body, even when your mind tries to push through. The cortisol. The elevated heart rate. The tightness in your chest that you've just learned to live with, because everything depends on you.

You are the provider. The protector. The nurturer. All wrapped into one body, one brain, one heart that barely gets a break. And even when you smile, even when the house is peaceful, that stress doesn't leave. It just gets quiet for a minute. But it's still sitting on your shoulders, reminding you that no one else is coming.

It's not just the stress inside the home, it's the pressure outside of it too. As single parents, we're constantly navigating a society that wasn't built with us in mind. The policies, the headlines, the rumors, it all adds up. Every time a new administration talks about cutting public housing, reducing SNAP benefits, or slashing childcare support, it feels like a personal attack. Like they don't see us. Like they assume we've already been helped, when in reality, the system still hasn't even acknowledged the full weight we carry.

There's always talk about two-parent households being "the goal," but what about the reality we're living right now? There's no surge of child support checks rolling in. There's no co-parent coming through consistently. And yet, the benefits they want to take away are the ones holding up entire families.

It's hard to breathe under that kind of pressure. Hard to plan. Hard to feel safe. Because at any moment, it feels like something else might be pulled out from under you.

No matter what they cut, no matter who shows up or who doesn't, you have to keep showing up. For your kids. For yourself. For your future. Because as long as you're there, the house will be covered. These children will be loved. Their minds will be poured into. Their talents will be noticed. Their dreams will be protected.

I don't wait around for someone else to validate my effort. I see it in my kids. In their brilliance. In their joy. In the way they speak with confidence and curiosity. That's how I know I'm doing a good job. That's how I measure success. I'm not just surviving, I'm building something. Even when it's hard. Even when it's invisible. Even when no one is clapping. I'm handling my business, loving myself, and nurturing every part of this life with purpose. Because they deserve it. And so do I.

So no, I'm not bitter. I'm not broken. I'm not waiting for rescue. I'm raising futures. I'm rewriting normal. I'm showing my children what strength really looks like, not loud and flashy, but steady, faithful, and rooted in love. You might not see the stress on my face. You might not hear the conversations I have with God late at night. But make no mistake, the work is being done. The legacy is being built. And even if I'm doing it in the shadows, I promise you it's radiant.

Chapter 45

Balancing Budgets, Breaking Families

Under the Trump administration, significant cuts were proposed to child welfare programs. For instance, the House Republican budget plan aimed to slash Medicaid and food assistance, reallocating funds toward tax breaks for the wealthy. This approach will severely impact low-income families, including single-parent households. Additionally, the administration has changed laws as it pertains to education, and restrictions surrounding Section 8. These proposed reductions will have many children without essential support services.

In recent years, Republican lawmakers, especially during Trump's presidency, have pushed for deep cuts to programs that working-class and single-parent families rely on just to stay afloat. We're talking about Medicaid, SNAP (food stamps), and even housing support. They put forward budget plans that would take billions away from these services, only to funnel the savings into tax breaks for the ultra-wealthy. And it wasn't just a small trim. Recent policy changes and reconstructed laws have put most families in a vulnerable position. There is an increasing uncertainty with access to higher educational opportunities and programs with every new bill passed.

That kind of move doesn't just hurt numbers on a spreadsheet. It hurts households like mine. It tells single mothers, "We don't see you. We don't care that you're raising children alone. Figure it out." But the truth is, we have been figuring it out. With or without their support.

In 2022, nearly 16 million children under 18 lived with their mothers only. These children are more likely to experience poverty compared to those in married-parent families, leading to adverse effects on their health and education.

Additionally, in 2023, 38.7% of households with incomes below the federal poverty line were food insecure. Single-parent households, particularly those headed by women, are disproportionately affected by food insecurity, impacting their overall well-being.

I've been fortunate enough to have a strong support system, family that steps in when they can, shoulders I can lean on. But let me be clear: even with that, it's still hard. It still takes everything I've got. Now imagine the mothers out here who don't have anyone to call, who are truly doing it all on their own.

When nearly forty percent of low-income households are food insecure, it's not because people are lazy or irresponsible, it's because the system is built to let us fall through the cracks. Constantly increasing food prices affect everyone in this economy. When the government pulls back support, it's like pulling the rug out from under families already trying to balance on one foot.

SNAP isn't just some extra bonus, it's survival. It's groceries when the paycheck's already gone. The cost of living all across the U.S has risen sharply in the last 10 years. Sometimes it's the reason your child can open the fridge and still find something to eat at the end of the month. So, when politicians push for stricter work requirements or try to limit how long you can get benefits, they're not creating accountability, they're creating crisis.

TANF is supposed to be a temporary safety net, but there are hoops people have to jump through just to qualify. And even when you get it, the monthly amount is barely enough to cover a single bill. They say it's about encouraging work, but what it really encourages is burnout, shame, and desperation.

There have recently been changes in regards to Section 8. There is a stigma that comes with it. People love to act like housing assistance is a handout for the lazy, like the folks receiving it are just sitting around doing nothing. That couldn't be further from the truth.

Many people on Section 8 do work. They're holding down jobs, sometimes multiple, but they still can't afford full market rent. That's the real issue. Wages haven't kept up with the cost of living, and housing prices are ridiculous in most cities. So, Section 8 isn't some luxury, it's a lifeline. And cutting funding or limiting access just makes the burden even heavier for families already trying to stay afloat.

At the end of the day, we're not asking for luxury, we're asking for fairness. For dignity. For a system that actually supports the families it claims to protect. These cuts and rollbacks? They don't just balance budgets. They break people. And yet, we keep going. We show up. We raise these babies, juggle jobs, and stretch every dollar like magic. But it shouldn't take a miracle to make it through the month. And the truth is, no matter how strong we are, nobody should have to do it all with the odds stacked this high.

Chapter 46

Double Standards, Single Mothers

Let me be real: if I, as a mother, walked off and left my child without food, without clothes, without a roof, I'd be in jail. Neglect. Abandonment. I'd be labeled unfit. But when fathers do it, when they walk off and disappear, nobody bats an eye. The system shrugs. Society looks away. They say, "Well, he left the kids with their mother," like that magically makes it okay.

Then, here come the narratives painting mothers as angry, bitter, manipulative. But let me ask this, why are the women the ones showing up consistently. A lot of these women treat your children really well. Isn't it worth sacrificing for the good of your children. We don't like lying to our children for you, but absent fathers often label truth as slander. But it is imperative that mothers are truthful with their children once they reach a certain age. If a mother does not honestly answer questions after her child reaches a certain age, she is jeopardizing her kids trust and future relationship with them.

Here's what I've seen too many times: when the relationship ends, the father takes everything he considers his. His clothes, his shoes, his TV, maybe even his dog. Everything he feels entitled to. But what he doesn't fight for, what he doesn't claim with the same urgency, is the child. Eventually that comes to the surface. Kids can see that for themselves.

The child gets left behind like an afterthought. Like a shared memory of a relationship gone wrong, instead of a living, breathing human being who still needs both parents to show up. And co-parenting? That often isn't even on the table. Because when the love fades, so does the responsibility for them. Not for us. We're the ones who stay. We're the ones who pick up the pieces and keep it moving.

Chapter 47

Legal Double Standard:

Legally, mothers are held to a completely different standard. If we miss school pickups, can't provide, or get caught in a rough patch, there are caseworkers, court dates, and threats of losing custody. The system is quick to punish us if we fall short. Often bitter fathers, and a predatory government is just waiting for a woman to fall into a vulnerable position.

But for fathers? For non-custodial parents who don't pay support or don't show up consistently? The consequences are weak, if they come at all. You can rack up thousands in unpaid support and still walk around untouched. There are no police knocking at your door for emotional neglect. There's no urgency. No money. Just excuses. And that legal silence

reinforces a cultural one.

Chapter 48

Emotional Double Standard:

Then there's the emotional weight. Society expects mothers to be superheroes. We're supposed to carry the financial load, the emotional burden, the discipline, the nurturing, and the healing, all while staying gracious, peaceful, and unbothered.

When fathers do the bare minimum, maybe a visit here, a text there, they're praised like they deserve a trophy. "At least he came around." "At least he's trying." That kind of energy sends a loud message: men get credit for showing up, while women get criticized no matter what.

We're told not to complain. Not to be "bitter." But the truth is, this isn't about bitterness. It's about balance. And for too long, the scales have been tipped in silence. This isn't just a parenting issue; it's a justice issue. A moral one. We've created a culture where one parent is expected to give everything while the other can give nothing and still be seen as a parent. That's not co-parenting. That's exploitation.

We need to stop normalizing abandonment just because it's dressed up in silence. We need to stop telling mothers to "be strong" while we let fathers be absent without consequence. And we need to start holding both parents to the same standard, legally, emotionally, and financially. Children deserve more. Mothers deserve more. The whole family structure deserves truth, accountability, and protection, not just when it's convenient.

So, here's the call: if you're a parent, be one. In action, not just in name. In consistency, not just in DNA. Financially, because it takes real money and real time to care for these children. Because these kids didn't ask to be born, but they do deserve to be fully loved, fully supported, and never left holding half the family while the other half disappears.

By leaving over $11 billion in child support unpaid each year, we're not just failing families, we're failing our economy. In 2017, custodial parents were owed over $30 billion but only received about 62 percent of it. That's nearly $11 billion missing from household budgets. When those payments don't come through, that mother has to supplement the fathers portion of payment from her own money. That further tightens the financial budget for her creating an atmosphere in which her money cannot thrive or invest in their children's future.

Here's what happens when child support does flow as it's supposed to: It injects money directly into the economy. For every dollar delivered to a child's household through proper child support, that family spends it on food, clothing, utilities, and school supplies, keeping local businesses thriving. That money isn't just child's support, it's economic stimulus. But when it's unpaid, families absorb the loss, and local economies feel it too. More emergencies, more debt, more community strain.

Think about equity across financial responsibilities. When we hold non-custodial parents accountable, we do more than support kids, we strengthen families and communities. Enforcing child support isn't just legal, it's economic justice. It's saying, "Your child deserves stability. You are part of this."

So, what do we do with this truth? We stop treating unpaid child support like a family drama, and start addressing it as a national issue. Because it is. We need stronger enforcement systems that don't just file paperwork, but actually track, collect, and distribute what's owed. We need to close the loopholes that let people dodge responsibility while children go without. And we need to shift the narrative, because this isn't about punishing parents. It's about protecting children. When both parents are held accountable, everyone benefits. Children thrive. Families stabilize. Communities grow. That's what happens when support becomes a shared responsibility instead of a solo burden.

Global models: How Economic Fairness Fuels Nation-Building

Global Comparison: China vs. United States

Since the late nineteen seventies, China has sustained some of the fastest economic growth in modern history. Averaging around ten percent annual GDP growth from 1978 to 2005, and still hitting nearly nine percent growth per year through the nineties and early 2000s. Its GDP has ballooned from under four hundred billion US dollars in 1978 to over eighteen trillion in 2023 .

By comparison, the US economy grew steadily from about five hundred billion dollars in 1960 to well over twenty-two trillion USD by 2023 . That's impressive. The growth pattern differs: China's strategy centered on massive state investment, family-supportive social systems, and industrial expansion. Whereas the U.S. relied more on market forces and individual initiative, with minimal national investment into caregiving or parental support.

We've learned to call it "love" when women overextend and "sacrifice" when they burn themselves out. But when men withdraw, we call it space, freedom, or healing. The truth is, those emotional double standards don't end at the heart, they reach the wallet. They decide who pays, who repairs, and who rebuilds when the relationship ends.

Chapter 49

Money Matters

At some point, women stop talking about co-parenting and start talking about money. Not because love disappeared, but because reality showed up. Co-parenting sounds collaborative. Equal time, equal effort, and shared priorities, but too often it's an illusion built on unspoken inequities. One parent is at the school, the doctor, the grocery store, and there for the late-night emergencies. The other sends a text or two and calls it effort. When the invisible load starts to feel unbearable, the conversation shifts from partnership to provision. From "we" to "me."

When you're the one paying for everything, physically, mentally, and emotionally, money matters. It matters when the light bill is due. When your child's shoes don't fit. When the field-trip permission slip needs cash by Friday and you've already stretched last week's paycheck to make it happen. It matters when survival turns into strategy and love becomes labor measured in receipts.

Women aren't asking for money out of greed. They're asking because they've already given everything else. Time. Sleep. Energy. Sanity. And money. They're asking for accountability in a system that rarely enforces it. They're asking for responsibility from the other parent.

The system proves the point. Some mothers are awarded as little as $25 a month in court-ordered child support. That's barely enough for a single pack of diapers or a few gallons of milk. Meanwhile, other non-custodial parents owe $25,000 to $50,000 in back pay and face no real consequence. The laws meant to protect children often protect neglect instead.

The imbalance is staggering: some are punished and ostracized for needing help, while others are rewarded for withholding it. The parent who shows up daily is scrutinized; the one who doesn't is excused. And when the custodial parent finally sets a boundary or stops begging, she's labeled bitter, angry, or money hungry. But the truth is simpler than the stereotypes: Money matters because consistency costs. Being there everyday cost.

Every child deserves the security of a home that isn't hanging on by a thread. Every parent doing the heavy lifting deserves more than lip service. The courts talk about "the best interest of the child," but if the child's best interest doesn't include economic stability, what kind of interest is that? It's not about revenge, it's about responsibility.

Until policy reflects the true cost of raising a child, we'll keep pretending that $25 and a weekend visit makes a family whole. We'll keep calling survival "support" and injustice "equal." Because in America's child-support system, love is optional, but money is the only language the law listens to. The math doesn't lie.

According to the U.S. Department of Agriculture, it costs over $310,000 to raise a child to age eighteen when you factor in food, housing, education, health care, and basic needs. That's before inflation, before extracurriculars, before emergencies. Every year, those numbers climb, but child-support orders haven't kept pace with the cost of living. A basic fast-food meal for a family of three now costs around $40. Sit down at a modest restaurant and you're spending $65 to $100 for one meal. That's for one night. One dinner. And kids don't just eat once. They eat three to four times a day, and they need snacks.

Then there's everything else. The quiet expenses that never make the headlines: earphones that need replacing every semester because school assignments are now online; software updates, internet subscriptions, lunch accounts, lost jackets, birthday parties, field trips, new sneakers, therapy sessions, sports fees, and hair appointments. Each item might look small, but together they build a constant mountain of invisible costs.

These aren't luxuries—they're the baseline requirements of raising a child in the digital age. The economic updates that mothers can't skip, but fathers often can, because the world doesn't hold them accountable for missing the small things that matter most.

If a man wants to live with a roommate, he can. If

he wants to disconnect the internet to save money, he can. If he decides to skip dinner and hustle on self-improvement for a few months, he can. Freedom, for him, is a financial option. But a mother doesn't have that choice. She can't unplug the Wi-Fi because her child needs it for homework. She can't just live anywhere to save on rent because she's thinking about safety, predators, and peace of mind. She can't skip groceries without teaching her child the language of lack. Every decision she makes is filtered through protection and provision.

When the bills stack higher than her income, the consequences don't fall on her alone, they fall on her children. One skipped payment becomes one more chipped piece of stability. A missed field trip. A quiet embarrassment in the lunch line. A lesson in going without that no child should have to learn.

Meanwhile, non-custodial parents with overdue

balances can build new lives without consequence. Some owe $25,000 to $50,000 in back support yet still buy cars, start businesses, even remarry, while the custodial parent faces judgment for asking the court to enforce what's already owed. The child-support system doesn't just reflect inequality, it manufactures it. It creates two economies: one of freedom and one of survival. One parent gets to rebuild; the other has to hold everything together. And when the system lets one side opt out, the other pays in full, not just in dollars, but in dignity, exhaustion, and dreams deferred. That's why money matters. Because money isn't just currency, it's care, consistency, and consequence. And until policy starts valuing the full cost of care work, mothers will keep carrying the deficit the system refuses to see.

What no one wants to talk about is how this stress lives in a woman's body. You can't carry years of financial strain, emotional neglect, and constant vigilance without it leaving a mark. The body remembers every overdue bill, every missed hour of sleep, every time she held her breath trying to stretch $50 into a week's worth of groceries. This is more than exhaustion, it's erosion.

Women who shoulder the full weight of single parenthood experience higher rates of hypertension, strokes, heart disease, cancer, and autoimmune disorders. Studies show that chronic stress and economic insecurity shorten lifespans, weaken immune systems, and turn survival into sickness. And when that sickness comes, guess who pays? The mother. Her children. Her health. Her peace. She pays with doctor visits, prescriptions, unpaid time off, and medical debt that spirals for years. The same system that ignored her struggle now profits from her illness, through healthcare premiums, pharmaceutical sales, and hospital bills.

What begins as neglect turns into a business model.

Every uncollected dollar in child support becomes another dollar the government earns through interest, debt, or disease. It's an economy built on burnout. Meanwhile, the men who abandoned responsibility get to keep breathing easy, untouched by the physical consequences of their choices. They walk free while the mothers of their children are dying slow, invisible deaths, slow, torturous murders by stress, by poverty, by policy.

The world praises women for being strong, but strength was never supposed to mean self-destruction. The world calls it resilience, but what it really is, is survival in a system designed to wear her down until she breaks. And yet she rises. Every morning, she still rises. They tell single mothers, "money isn't everything." But the moment we ask for it for our kids, the world starts preaching patience. If money isn't everything, then pay what you owe. Run it back.

Some of these men have been on five-year vacations from fatherhood, untouched by accountability while mothers have worked double shifts, skipped meals, and cried in silence just to make life look easy for their children. The truth is, that money was never for us, it was for them. For the children who didn't ask to carry the cost of another adult's absence. For the groceries, the rent, the utilities, the school supplies, the therapy sessions, the peace of mind.

Every dollar unpaid becomes another hour the mother has to work. Every hour she works becomes another moment stolen from her child. That's not independence, it's exploitation. And when the system lets it slide, it sends a message: that women's labor is optional, that fathers' absence is forgivable, and that a child's wellbeing is negotiable.

Meanwhile, the same men who say "money isn't everything" somehow find enough of it to fund new relationships, trips, and new hobbies. Their debts don't disappear, they just get buried under the backs of the women who keep paying both halves of the bill. If the roles were reversed, she'd be living comfortably too. But instead, she's paying for his half, his absence, his pride.

Let's call it what it is: control. A twisted form of dominance dressed up as detachment. A God complex that feeds on her exhaustion and mistakes power for punishment. There's a kind of control that masquerades as manhood. A counterfeit authority that confuses dominance with divine order. It's a God complex that feeds on her exhaustion, growing stronger every time she's too tired to argue, too worn down to demand fairness. It mistakes power for punishment and leadership for leverage. It doesn't want partnership; it wants proof that she'll keep carrying what he refuses to lift. The tragedy is that this isn't strength, it's dependency in disguise. Because without someone to bear the weight, his illusion of power collapses. True authority uplifts; false authority drains. And too many women have been sacrificed at the altar of a man's insecurity dressed up as Godhood.

But here's the shift:
Women are done carrying that illusion.
We are done paying double for someone else's lesson.
We are done letting neglect disguise itself as freedom.

If money isn't everything, then prove it by paying what's owed. Because for too long, the system has protected comfort over accountability, ego over equity, and men over motherhood. Money matters, not because we worship it, but because our children deserve it. Because stability is sacred. Because love without support is just another lie we're tired of living through.

The truth is, this imbalance doesn't exist in a vacuum, it's a reflection of a nation in transition. The family structure America was built on no longer mirrors the families who actually live within it. Women are leading households, redefining provision, and rebuilding community without the safety nets or support systems they were promised. Yet the laws, policies, and cultural expectations around family haven't evolved to match that reality. The question is no longer whether the American family has changed, it's whether America itself is willing to change with it.

Chapter 50

America's Shifting Family Structure

In the 1960s, around nine percent of U.S. children were raised in single-parent homes. Fast forward to the present and it's nearly thirty percent. That means nearly one in three children today lives with just one parent, and in eighty percent of those cases, it's their mother. Meanwhile, countries that invest more deeply in family welfare, while not perfect, show higher levels of social stability and collective economic growth.

Chapter 51

Bridge to Call-To-Action

1. Childhood Poverty Rates & Single Parent Households

Nearly one in six children in the U.S.—about sixteen percent—live below the poverty line. Digging deeper, almost thirty percent of children in single-parent homes face poverty, compared to just six percent in two-parent households. That gap isn't just numbers, it's life on the line. These are homes where meals are skipped, bills go unpaid, and stress becomes the baseline. Poverty isn't an event for these children; it's an atmosphere they're forced to breathe.

2. Educational Impact & Long-Term Outcomes

Children growing up in single-parent households face systemic barriers that show up early and compound over time. Lower test scores, higher dropout rates, and reduced college attendance aren't rare anomalies—they're *symptoms* of policy failure. Material deprivation, reduced emotional support, and frequent household transitions all contribute. When debris of economic instability hits a child, their opportunity shrinks—and so does our collective future.

3. Biological & Psychological Toll of Poverty

It's not just about wallets; it's also about health. Children in poverty may face accelerated biological aging, with elevated stress markers and shorter telomeres, meaning years taken off their cellular lifespan. The long-term impacts include higher rates of chronic illness, mental health disorders, and delayed cognitive development. These aren't life storms; they're structural storms, policies, and neglect beating down on vulnerable children from day one.

If America wants to stay competitive on the world stage technologically, economically, even militarily, it has to start by investing in its children. Other nations have already learned what America refuses to see: when you invest in families, you invest in safety. In China, for instance, the intentional homicide rate in 2020 was approximately 0.50 per 100,000 people, according to World Bank data—one of the lowest in the world. The rate has even declined by about 3.22% from 2019 to 2020. That's not coincidence, it's correlation. When families are fed, housed, and supported, communities are calmer. Economic security reduces violence, and collective care becomes its own form of national defense. We say we want to be the best. We say we want innovation, progress, excellence. But you can't build a nation of inventors, scientists, and leaders if you're starving the kids who are supposed to become them.

Investing in children isn't just a moral responsibility, it's a national strategy. Other nations know this. That's why they're pouring money into education, nutrition, family support, and long-term childhood development. Because a healthy, stable child today becomes a creative, contributing adult tomorrow. But here? We let millions of children grow up with unstable housing, underfunded schools, and overburdened parents and then wonder why we're falling behind in science, math, and innovation. You cannot build rockets with broken childhoods. You can't lead the future when your future is struggling to eat breakfast.

If we're serious about being a strong nation, then we have to start treating the well-being of children, and the parents raising them, as a matter of national priority. Not just a private issue. Not just "her problem." Our collective future

depends on how we treat our children right now.

Chapter 52

Call to Action: A New Paradigm for American Families

It's time to shift the story. For too long, we've framed single motherhood as a failure, child support as a punishment, and poverty as a personal flaw. If we want to build a stronger America, we have to tell a different story. One rooted in shared responsibility, compassion, truth, and strategic investment.

We need to stop asking, "Why didn't they try harder?" and start asking, "What systems failed them?" We need to move from shame to support, from blame to building. Because every child, no matter who raised them, deserves a nation that believes in their potential.

A new American family structure is already here. Diverse, resilient, dynamic. What we need now is a new narrative to match it, and policies that reflect it. One built on inclusion, accountability, and care as infrastructure. Not with slogans, but with action.

Let's build a country that honors all labor of parenting. That values the lives of children. That stops treating families like a private burden and starts seeing them as the public treasure they are. Because a nation that invests in its families doesn't just survive, it thrives.

Chapter 53

The Cost of Ignoring Care Work

Care work holds up the world, but you wouldn't know it by looking at how we treat the people who do it. Raising children, supporting elders, managing daily life, holding space for others' growth all of it takes time, intention, energy, and emotional bandwidth. Yet society labels it "unpaid," "unskilled," or worse, "expected." Let's be clear: caregiving is labor. And it's massive.

In the U.S. alone, unpaid care work is worth over one trillion dollars every year, with women performing about two-thirds of it. Asian women and Latinas contribute the highest number of care hours per person—averaging 245 hours of caregiving a year. Globally, unpaid domestic and care work totals an estimated $10.8 trillion annually, or about 9% of global GDP. That's the equivalent of 16 billion hours of labor every single day. Roughly two billion full-time jobs, and women do nearly three times more of that work than men.

So, when that labor is done by a single mother? Multiply the intensity. Every ride to practice, every school meeting, every doctor's visit, every moment spent trying to stretch limited resources in the most strategic way, that's not just time. It's a physical and emotional investment in the next generation. It's not just nurturing, it's nation-building. But the system doesn't treat it that way.

When we ignore care work, we ignore the backbone of the economy. We strain families and exhaust our most essential workers, mothers, grandmothers, aunties, caregivers, and community builders. The very people holding it all together.

Here's the part people don't want to talk about: when you ignore the weight of care work, when you dismiss the labor of motherhood, when you act like parenting is something women are just supposed to do without support—you create a culture where more and more women say, "No thanks." And can you blame them?

Motherhood shouldn't feel like a punishment. It shouldn't mean isolation, exhaustion, and economic instability. Yet women providing family care in the U.S. lose an estimated 15% of their lifetime earnings, that's nearly $295,000 per caregiver over a career. Meanwhile, family caregivers of older adults create roughly $873 billion worth of labor every year, almost entirely unpaid and unsupported.

When that kind of value is ignored, the consequences ripple outward. Fewer people choose to raise children. Your future workforce shrinks. Your caregiving systems collapse. The nation grows older without a new generation to sustain it. This is what happens when we treat care work as invisible: eventually, people stop doing it.

If we want strong families, strong communities, and a strong future, we must start treating care work like the foundation it is, not an afterthought, not a burden to be carried alone, but a shared responsibility. One that deserves time, resources, and respect. Because when you value the people who do the caring, you build a society that actually cares.

Let me be clear, being a parent is not a consequence. It's not a burden I regret. It's a role I cherish, even when it feels like the world doesn't cherish me in return. Parenthood, especially motherhood, is one of the most sacred, powerful, and creative acts a person can step into. But sacred doesn't mean easy. And powerful doesn't mean supported.

We love our children with everything we have. That love is what drives us. It's why we keep showing up, keep trying, keep sacrificing. But love shouldn't mean carrying it all alone. Love deserves backup. It deserves policy. It deserves rest.

So, the resolution is this: we honor the role, but we also demand respect. We celebrate the joy, but we tell the truth about the labor. And we insist that care work be seen, supported, and shared. Because raising a child isn't just a private act of love, it's a public act of building the future. And that deserves everything we've got.

Chapter 54

Restoring the Mother: Postpartum Care and the Price of Neglect

We talk a lot about childbirth in America, but we talk very little about what happens after. Once the baby is here, the mother disappears from the conversation. The focus shifts entirely to the child, while the woman who just carried, delivered, and now nurtures that life is left to recover alone.

Other countries have figured this out. In Japan, new mothers are given space to heal. Many stay in maternity care facilities for weeks, sometimes even a full month. They're monitored for postpartum depression, supported physically, fed, and rested. It's not a luxury. It's seen as necessary.

In contrast, American mothers are often sent home within 24 to 48 hours of delivery, expected to bounce back, care for a newborn, and in many cases, return to work within weeks. No check-ins. No emotional support. Just a quiet, invisible expectation to hold it all together.

Chapter 55

Key Postpartum Mental Health Stats

In the U.S., about one in seven new mothers, roughly 14 percent, experience postpartum depression (PPD), which is more serious than the two-week "baby blues" that about 50 to 85 percent of women go through. Yet many cases go undiagnosed and untreated. Around 60 percent of affected mothers never get a diagnosis, and half of those diagnosed don't receive treatment.

What's more, PPD isn't just in the early weeks. By nine to ten months postpartum, 7.2 percent of mothers report depressive symptoms. More than half weren't symptomatic earlier. That means the struggle can surface late, long after the hospital checkups are done.

Meanwhile, in Japan where postpartum care often includes a month of structured rest, research shows 14.3 percent of mothers experience PPD at one month postpartum . Despite that being similar to U.S. rates, Japanese mothers receive ongoing emotional support and medical monitoring in those early weeks, which researchers credit with helping reduce long-term impact.

Personal Reflection: Postpartum, Pain, and Survival

I know postpartum firsthand. I felt it after both of my children, but with my second son it hit hard. It wasn't just emotional, it was physical. Traumatic. And it was made worse by a system that showed me, in the most intimate moment of vulnerability, that it wasn't built to protect me. It was built to protect the doctors, the institutions.

They numbed me with a spinal tap, and then I had a cesarean. I needed a high dosage of medication for my body to numb, bring down my blood pressure, anxiety medicine, I was highly medicated. The next day, with that medication still wearing off, they took me to the shower and left me there alone. I specifically asked for a nurse to stay with me, for my safety, but I was ignored. And I fell.

That fall would go on to affect me for years. I hemorrhaged for over eighteen months. I was sick. I was exhausted. I was still going to work on the night shift, still up all night, still caring for my children during the daytime, while bleeding and barely holding myself together. I was married at the time, but I still felt alone in it. No rest. No space to heal. Just expectation.

When I tried to seek accountability for the fall, for the lack of support, for the damage, I hit a wall. There was no path for restitution. No system to say, "You deserved better." Just silence. Just survival. Postpartum depression doesn't always show up right away. Sometimes it comes in waves. Sometimes it hides behind responsibilities. And sometimes, it lingers long after your body has supposedly healed. That was my reality. I had to fight my way back, not just physically, but mentally, emotionally, spiritually.

I'm grateful to say I'm no longer in that place. But too many women are. And they're doing it quietly. While raising children. While holding down jobs. While wondering if they're ever going to feel like themselves again.

Chapter 56

Global Contrast: What Support Looks Like in Other Nations

What I went through wasn't rare in the U.S., but it should be. Because in other parts of the world, women are treated differently after giving birth. They're cared for. Protected. Respected. In countries like Japan, postpartum recovery is not left to chance or a woman's personal resilience. It's policy.

In Japan, many mothers stay in specialized postpartum care facilities for up to four weeks after delivery. These centers offer meals, medical checkups, emotional support, and round-the-clock care for both the mother and the newborn. It's a structured system designed to help prevent postpartum depression, not just treat it after the damage is done. And trust me, they are not going to treat you once the damage is done. The law was created to protect the doctors, and the hospitals, the institution, not the people.

Some European countries go even further. In the Netherlands, for example, new mothers receive home visits from a maternity nurse for the first eight to ten days after birth—helping with breastfeeding, household chores, and emotional adjustment. In Sweden, both parents receive paid leave up to 480 days per child, shared however the couple sees fit. That's not just about bonding, it's about stability.

Chapter 57

Reimagining Maternal Health: A Call for Change

It's time to stop treating postpartum recovery as an afterthought. It's time to stop asking mothers to bounce back, hold it all together, and pretend like nothing happened. We need a new standard, one that honors birth as a major life event, not just a medical transaction. One that provides time to rest, space to heal, and access to real support. Because when we care for mothers, we care for children. And when we care for children, we build the future.

This isn't just about maternal health, it's about national health. It's about creating systems that see women not as vessels, but as vital to the strength, stability, and success of a nation. Let's reimagine what it means to support life, not just in the womb, but in the world that comes after.

1. U.S. Unpaid Care Work Is a Trillion-Dollar Engine

Every year, Americans dedicate nearly 245 hours per person to unpaid caregiving. That's worth over one trillion dollars, with women alone contributing around $643 billion in invisible labor. Yet this essential infrastructure goes unrecognized and undervalued.

2. Shrinking the Workforce = Shrinking the Economy

By 2030, failing to support America's care system could shave $290 billion off our GDP annually. The equivalent to losing over half of our projected economic growth. At the same time, unpaid caregiving costs U.S. businesses $17 to 33 billion each year due to lost productivity.

3. Care Builds the Labor Market

When childcare gets more affordable, women join the

workforce more. A 10 percent reduction in childcare costs correlates with a 0.25 to 11 percent increase in maternal employment. Early education programs deliver $8.60 in returns for every dollar invested, helping families today and growing human capital tomorrow.

4. Care Benefits Employers Too

Companies that provide childcare support see up to 425 percent return on investment, thanks to better retention, productivity, and fewer disruptions. Meanwhile, 88 percent of small businesses agree their workforce would be more stable if caregiving was funded and accessible.

What This Means in Real Life:

Care work isn't charity. It's infrastructure. It's economic

strategy. When we treat caregiving as the national resource it is, we:

- Add a solid trillion dollars in domestic value

- Prevent $290 billion in GDP loss

- Unlock millions more workers, especially women, into the economy

- Stabilize businesses and communities

- Build tomorrow's workforce from the ground up

This isn't theoretical. It's a blueprint. For eons, Black communities have poured time, energy, and care into systems that rarely give anything back. From raising other people's children to nursing families, maintaining homes, and supporting churches and schools, our labor has always been essential, but never fully valued. Now it's time to change that.

By reclaiming care work and redefining it as our resource, our economy, and our path to wealth, we take the labor that's always been in us, and make it work for us. We create our own businesses. We build our own networks. We care for our own with dignity and sustainability. Because when we control the systems that care for us, we control our future.

Chapter 58

The Vision: Care as the Key to Collective Advancement

This is a call to refocus. We don't need to wait on billion-dollar tech or luxury industries to create change. We already have a trillion-dollar economy sitting in our kitchens, classrooms, and communities. We just need to recognize it. Fund it. Own it. Care is power. It's how we survive, how we nurture, how we lead.

If we want to heal a nation, strengthen families, and secure our legacy, it starts right here with the people who've been doing the work all along. I've been in a caregiving role since I was eighteen, maybe nineteen. Not by title, not by profession, but by love. By necessity. My maternal grandmother was diagnosed with stage 4 breast cancer, and I helped care for her until the end. Simultaneously, my paternal grandmother had a stroke and developed dementia. Her illness stretched over nearly a decade, and I was there for that too.

I know what it means to be a caregiver. I know what it feels like to watch someone you love change before your eyes and still show up, day after day, with strength you didn't know you had. I know what it means to pour yourself out emotionally, physically, spiritually, and still have to keep going because life doesn't pause for grief or fatigue.

I've been doing this work long before I had children. Long before it was labeled labor. Long before anyone asked how I was managing. And I know I'm not alone. Caregiving is human. It's sacred. It's something we will all need, whether at the beginning of life or near the end. And yet, we treat it like an afterthought, like it's soft, like it's small. But it's not small.

It's essential. And it's a market. It's a structure. It's an entire economy waiting to be honored.

If we could shift the way we think about care and stop seeing it as invisible, unworthy, or expected, we could shift policy. We could shift power. We could shift the future. Because in the end, caregiving isn't just a role. It's a revolution.

Chapter 59

Nature Knows the Assignment

Parenthood is sacred. It is not just a biological experience, it is a divine assignment. When we become parents, we are given the closest earthly opportunity to understand God's love, God's patience, and God's design. A mother is like God in the eyes of a child. As they grow, they learn better. But, we become the first image of what love and authority look like. And that power, whether wielded with grace or neglected, shapes a child's spirit for life.

From the moment a child is conceived, we are invited into a covenant: to nurture, to protect, to guide. And in doing so, we do not just raise children, we re-raise ourselves.

Parenthood becomes a mirror. We teach, but we are also learning. We protect, but we are also healing. We guide, but we are also being pulled deeper into our own growth.

The divine role of a father is just as powerful. Though he is not the portal, he carries the seed. His presence, or his absence, has the power to shape a child's perception of trust, stability, and the very nature of the divine. When a father neglects his sacred duty, children often spend their lives searching for something that has always been inside them. His presence is not optional. It is spiritual. It is generational. It is sacred.

Together, when two parents honor their roles, even without romantic partnership, they become a spiritual force. The Bible says, "Where two or more are gathered in My name, there I am in the midst." So, it is with parenting. When both mother and father invest in their child's spirit, mind, and future, God meets them there. The covenant is strengthened. The child becomes covered.

Parenthood is not about ego. It's not about who was hurt or who left. It's about removing ourselves from our own feelings long enough to serve the soul we were entrusted with. And it's a limited time offer, because children grow fast. What you stress about this year might not matter next year. Diapers turn to grade school. Formula becomes field trips. And if you're too busy being bitter or absent, you'll miss it all.

Absentee fathers are often out searching for meaning, for legacy, for identity, and all the while, they're walking away from the very thing that would've given them all of that and more. They're missing the assignment. They're missing their own harvest.

Chapter 60

Nature doesn't miss the assignment.

In the natural world, animals, insects, even plants are designed with structures that honor and protect the feminine. Bee colonies revolve around the queen. Wolf packs shield the female and the pups. In spider communities, in herds of elephants, and even among hippos, the systems are built to preserve the source of life. In many cases, only a few males are allowed within the group to prevent disruption and ensure balance. Nature knows how to protect what matters most. Humanity, somehow, forgot.

Patriarchy, ego, and imbalance have distorted the sacred. We've turned good into bad, and bad into good. We praise selfishness and ridicule sacrifice. We normalize broken homes and call spiritual wounds "independence." But if we look at nature, we'll see that creation still remembers the blueprint. The earth still honors the vessel that brings life. The universe still respects the balance. And maybe that's why things are shifting now.

If you were God, Source, or Mother Nature herself and you saw the world overusing resources, neglecting family, destroying sacred bonds, wouldn't you start cleansing too? Wouldn't you start wiping the board, purifying the space, waking people up? That's what this moment in history feels like: a great unraveling, a necessary correction. This is not just about child support. This is about spiritual alignment.

To the children: out of all the galaxies and timelines, God chose for you to be here, now, with us. You are not an accident. You are not a mistake. You beat millions to be born. You are a walking miracle, sent here to explore the world, to know God, and to live a life full of joy and purpose. God did not create you to suffer. God created you to live and live abundantly. Everything beautiful was made with you in mind. You are loved. You are needed. You are divine.

And if you're reading this as an adult, this blessing is still yours. You are not too old to be chosen, to be healed, or to be seen. The same divine hand that planted you as a child still holds you now. You are not forgotten. You are still worthy of joy, of peace, and of love. Nature knows the assignment. And it's time we remember it too.

Support is a multifaceted concept that extends far beyond mere financial assistance. It means to bear part of the weight and hold someone up, to provide not just the necessities of life, but also encouragement, approval, and a foundation for growth. True support means being actively invested in someone's success, providing a stable base from which they can thrive, and enduring alongside them through challenges. In essence, support is the invisible thread that connects us, allowing us to hold each other up and move forward together.

Every day is a new opportunity to make different choices, breaking away from old patterns of trauma and heartache and choosing healing and unity. If a parent feels they cannot bring positivity into their child's life, it's still crucial for them to accept financial responsibility and always act in the best interest of the child. For those protecting their children, it's about being proactive and making honorable choices that honor not just your children and lineage, but also yourself and your community.

I truly believe that we all play a small part in a very big picture, and that everyone we encounter and everything we do has an impact. When we choose to step up and embrace our role, we empower not only ourselves but also the community around us. I've been blessed to grow up in an environment where the men around me stepped up and helped the people around them. Seeing my father support so many people around him gave me a different perspective on manhood. It shaped how I view support and the standard of expectation that I have for myself.

There's no time like the present to embrace change and become the best version of ourselves. It doesn't cost a thing to be a good person, to shift our habits, and to step into a brighter, more positive way of living. We're alive in this moment, so let's seize the day and make the most of it. I hope that this piece of work provokes thought, healing, and a broader perspective of an ongoing underlying problem. With compromise, we can create fair solutions, policies, and fresh healthy perspectives that can create positive changes for everyone across a large economic scale. The power of change lies within us all, and it is our responsibility to harness that power to create a positive impact! I believe that it is time for everyone to take their place. To share equitable responsibility and accountability to balance an unfair system that we have perpetuated and supported. This is not a topic that is talked about on national platforms, but it is time that we have the conversation.

Chapter 61

Final Words

I believe this is the beginning of a new dialogue, a new awareness, and a new direction. Whether you read this as a parent, a policymaker, or a person simply trying to understand, thank you for being here. The systems may be broken, but we are not. We rise not just by surviving, but by demanding better, building stronger, and choosing to see one another.

We are the village. We are the voice. And always remember, love leads, truth frees, and power builds.

And to all the single mothers out there, I am proud of you. You are graduating, getting certified, and passing classes. You are getting healthy, changing habits, and investing into your futures. A lot of you are saving money, buying houses, and building a beautiful life that you should be proud of. Don't ever stop striving or stop growing. Keep becoming! Keep shining as the main character in your life story.

THE ART OF ESHE

About the Author

Eshe Oluchi is a writer, visionary, and founder of *The Art of Eshe*, a creative and spiritual brand devoted to healing, truth, and transformation. Through her work, she explores the intersections of policy, parenthood, and purpose—revealing how personal stories shape collective systems. *The Child Support Deficit* grew from her own lived experience and her deep commitment to restoring dignity, empathy, and balance in conversations about family and care.

Rooted in faith and fueled by resilience, Eshe's voice bridges the spiritual and the social, reminding readers that provision is more than a paycheck, it's a promise to one another.